The Immigration Mystique

ALSO BY CHILTON WILLIAMSON JR.

NONFICTION

Saltbound: A Block Island Winter

Roughnecking It

FICTION

Desert Light

The Homestead

The Immigration Mystique

America's False Conscience

CHILTON WILLIAMSON JR.

BasicBooks
A Division of HarperCollins*Publishers*

Designed by Elliott Beard

Library of Congress Cataloging-in-Publication Data
Williamson, Chilton.
    The immigration mystique : America's false conscience
/ by Chilton Williamson, Jr.
        p.   cm.
    Includes bibliographical references (p.   ) and index.
    ISBN 0–465–03286–9
    1. United States—Emigration and immigration—
Government policy.   2. United States—Emigration and
immigration—History.   I. Title.
JV6483.W55   1996
325.73'09—dc20   96-3841

---

96 97 98 99 00 ❖/HC 9 8 7 6 5 4 3 2 1

For Jennifer Lucas,
who let me know when she liked
something I wrote

Who would call in a
        foreigner—unless
an artisan with skill to
        serve the realm,
a healer, or a prophet, or
        a builder,
or one whose harp and song
        might give us joy.
All these are sought for on the
        endless earth,
but when have beggars come by
        invitation?
                —*From the* Odyssey
                trans. by Robert Fitzgerald

Contents

	Preface	xi
	Acknowledgments	xvii
I	The Unwelcome Debate	1
II	From Myth to Mystique	19
III	Mystique or Mistake?	81
	Conclusion: The Failure of American Immigration	193

Preface

As a magazine editor and contributor, I have spent a good deal of time in the last twenty years reading and commenting on the literature produced in reaction to America's latest immigration crisis, which has been developing since the early 1970s. In spite of the rare article, essay, or book—usually appearing in a marginal forum—keeping abreast of this flood of printed material has been for the most part a dispiriting and intensely frustrating business. Critics and defenders alike of our present immigration policy (or absence thereof) agree that the annual arrival of more than a million legal immigrants, compounded by several hundred thousand illegal ones, in the United States since 1990 is among the most significant events in the nation's history. The immigration debate of the 1980s and '90s may fairly be said to rank with the sectional argument that preceded the Civil War, the disagreements between interventionists and isolationists during the 1930s, and the moral and political upheavals created by the civil rights movement in the 1950s and '60s. Yet fully two decades of passionate, indignant, and frequently irritable commentary and advocacy, cutting across party and ideological lines, have failed to inspire public discussion at intellectual and rhetorical levels comparable to those attained in the course of earlier national crises—including the thirty-year furor over immigration that spanned the turn of the last century and had its fulfillment in the restrictionist legislation of the 1920s. In this sense, any patriotic gore to have been spilled, along with floods of ink, in the present controversy is thin indeed, in spite of all the sound and interesting work produced on the many subjects entwined with immigration, such as ethnicity and ethnic conflict, nationality and citizenship, migration and environmental carrying capacity, situational ethics, and international freedom of movement. While immigration—like slavery, racial separation, abortion, and environmentalism—is at bottom a moral issue, not a policy option, so far it has not succeeded in commanding the moral and intellectual rigor it demands.

The modern American disposition is to treat every public issue as fundamentally a problem in technique: a mechanical hitch in a technological society remediable by the application of more technique, as determined by still more technological consideration. And because Western society since before the Enlightenment has increasingly put technique in service to political economy, correctly described by the environmental philosopher Max Oelschlaeger as an acceptedly divine paradigm articulated through utilitarian individualism, in the West the logic of technique expresses itself in the language of economics, on the subject of immigration as on all others. Therefore, at the level of what passes for serious public debate, immigrationists and anti-immigrationists, liberals, conservatives, and moderates, have—until lately, anyway—confined themselves largely to the economic argument: Immigration increases, immigration does not increase but rather decreases, American prosperity, as measured by the gross domestic product and econometric standards of efficiency.

The rather offensive superficiality of the discussion that necessarily results is an evasion, rather than a denial, of the essentially moral nature of the problems posed by immigration. So also is the moralism of the American media, including the nation's most august newspapers, when they are compelled by events to address an issue that they prefer not to mention at all. Happy talk about the Statue of Liberty, a Nation of Immigrants, and the First Universal Nation, like expert talk about the Global Economy and hundreds of millions of human widgets or what Wayne Lutton, a contemporary student of immigration, calls growth blobs, is substantially a cover woven to conceal the desperate need for hard thinking and plain speaking on a number of related issues that most Americans above the social level of daytime drinkers in a roadside tavern have been taught to ignore, deny, or at least never to discuss—including, especially, matters pertaining to race, ethnicity, alienness, and national self-interest, all of them logically inseparable from the subject of immigration, frankly considered. So far as the debate can be restricted to economic concerns, it can be kept respectable; as long as it is confinable to the recitation of platitudes, half-truths, and even lies, it remains "well intentioned." Insofar as it is both, it continues to maintain the moralistic high ground.

But maintaining moralistic heights is not the same thing as thinking, and it certainly is not the same thing as thinking morally. In fact, it does hardly more than perform a variety of more or less elaborate emotional exercises and moralistic posturings. Americans for two hundred years have believed their country to be the special favorite of God; even today, amid waves of secularism washing over the United States like grand tsunamis, nearly 90 percent of American citizens claim to believe in the Divinity, still for the most part as He is understood by Christianity. Americans are said to have a conscience, as consequently America itself does: They, and it, are aggrieved by the plight of hosts of miserable people suffering famine, deprivation, and persecution in foreign lands, for whom the claims of conscience demand a ready welcome to America's shores—reflexively, and without account of cost. Accepting them here, the moralist argument concludes, is our most hallowed and long-standing tradition as a people. In addition to which, it also brings us incalculable economic rewards and benefits.

Of course, there is no gainsaying conscience, one of the most fundamental, unique, and therefore precious of human attributes. But in addition to conscience we have been invested with reason, among whose functions is to prevent moral ideas from lapsing into moralistic spasms, and to train thoughts up from spasms. The phenomenon of immigration has confronted the American people from 1609 to the present, yet—as generations of writers involved with the subject have noted—very little, if anything, of importance has been added to the substance of the debate, pro or con, since early times. In 1913 the sociologist Henry Pratt Fairchild identified four moral standpoints from which in his opinion the conscientious American observer must consider immigration: (1) that of the United States of America; (2) that of the sending countries; (3) that of the immigrants themselves; and (4) that of "humanity in general." To this at the close of the twentieth century the environmentalist concern for the carrying capacity of the nation's landmass needs to be appended. Professor Fairchild's assessment of the dimensions of immigration as a moral problem, by contrast with the postliterate message annealed with the news photographer's thirty-second footage of a ragged Zapotec Indian struggling across the border from Mexico and falling into the arms of a waiting Border Patrol agent, is infinitely more complex, grave, and weighted. It is also infinitely more moral. Finally, it is genuinely conscientious, in a way that the other makes only a pretense of being.

I make no claim with this book to say anything "new" about immigration to America, which has been described and debated almost exhaustively, but rather to recombine what happened, and what has previously been said of what happened, into new patterns, pointing not so much to new conclusions as to old conclusions differently understood. In so doing, I have taken the liberty of quoting liberally from other writers, both contemporary and historical, for the purpose of creating for the reader a sense of the protracted debate. My interest is to demonstrate with this book that the immigration problem, today as yesterday, is better addressed by insights taken from moral and religious philosophy, from history and international relations, and, most recently, from the science of ecology than by those appropriated from political economy, econometrics, and the sentimentalities of the mass media, to say nothing of politicians. I hope to suggest also a means of approaching the subject that subordinates utilitarianism, materialism, individualism, and moralism to community, the nation-state, national identity, and the terrible topics of the future of humanity and of the natural world itself. Finally, I wish to indicate a resolution to the American immigration crisis that—or so it seems to me—follows logically from this approach.

15 August 1995
Kemmerer, Wyoming

Acknowledgments

THE AUTHOR WISHES TO THANK THE FOLLOWING PERSONS for their contributions to the publication of this book: Tony Outhwaite of the JCA Literary Agency in New York City; Kermit Hummel, President and Publisher of Basic Books, Christopher Korintus, and Richard Fumosa of Basic; and Thomas Fleming, editor of *Chronicles: A Magazine of American Culture,* Wayne Lutton, and John H. Tanton, associate editor and editor, respectively, of the *Social Contract,* who read the manuscript and made useful suggestions for its improvement.

I

THE UNWELCOME DEBATE

M ORE THAN IN ITS PREVIOUS ERUPTIONS IN AMERICAN history, the immigration debate today is the unwelcome debate. In the late nineteenth and early twentieth centuries, public argument on the subject was carried on with candid vigor and a genuine enthusiasm for addressing large, unaccommodating, but nevertheless critical matters of vital import for the future of the United States. One hundred years later that vigor and enthusiasm are absent, as happens inevitably when participants on both sides of a very public disagreement are made nervous at the prospect of not being understood properly, and still more so by the possibility that they will be understood entirely.

As Professor Fairchild noted more than eighty years ago, the restrictionist party to the debate is morally disadvantaged by what he called "the indifference argument," which holds that immigrants, though not needed, nevertheless do the country no harm, and should therefore be accepted here if they wish to come. By denying this proposition, Fairchild observed, restrictionists assume the full burden of proof to the contrary and thereby risk being made to look meanspirited and selfish. Nowadays, the law of an unwritten sensitivity code induces nearly all commentators of whatever political persuasion to refer in passing to the "difficult choices" that everyone must make before taking a stand on the immigration question. Even so assured and disdainful a critic as George Kennan, who favors restriction, inclines his head toward "the delicate and difficult subject of immigration"; while Richard D. Lamm, a former Democratic governor of Colorado and an outspoken proponent of immigration reform, protests that he, like most

Americans, given their own immigrant roots and humanitarian traditions, regrets the necessity to limit immigration. Thomas Fleming, editor of the conservative journal *Chronicles: A Magazine of American Culture,* has suggested that overhaul of America's immigration policy was the greatest national issue of Ronald Reagan's presidency but one which failed to coalesce owing to a number of reasons, among them the Reagan administration's solicitousness for the agricultural industry of southern California and the rest of the Southwest, the openness of many of its staff to doctrines associated with global democracy and freedom of international movement, and its pronounced Pollyannaism and inertia. Probably the chief cause, however, was a simple reluctance on the part of the administration to reopen a controversy that it perceived to be at best unpleasant, at worst politically messy. Indeed, it is astonishing to watch the lengths to which politicians will go to avoid either discussing or dealing with the crisis of immigration, which they deny is a crisis in the first place. William French Smith, Reagan's attorney general, acknowledging blandly in 1982 that the United States had lost control of its borders, appeared entirely unaware that his statement was an astonishing admission on the part of a senior official in the government of the world's greatest superpower.[1] But the announcement in the summer of 1994 by Louis B. Freeh, President Clinton's director of the Federal Bureau of Investigation, that the bureau was preparing to open a branch in Moscow suggests better than anything the determination of the American government, whether controlled by the Democratic or the Republican Party, to sidestep the issue of immigration. The Moscow bureau would be required, Freeh stated, to help control international terrorism, theft, and fraud, and to protect the United States against their impingement upon national security. What the director did not explain was why an FBI bureau in Moscow is a cheaper, more efficient, and more effective means to safeguard America from Egyptian bombers and Nigerian credit-card sharks than enhanced restrictions on immigration to this country, as well as more stringent efforts to apprehend aliens who overstay their visas, would be.

The unwelcome debate is also, in a very real sense, the unnecessary debate. Historically, immigration has been unpopular with the American people and it remains so today, as one public-opinion survey after another registers the desire of an overwhelming majority of Americans for its drastic curtailment. A Columbia Broadcasting System poll conducted in 1994 found that two-thirds of those who want immigration quotas reduced prefer to see them abolished altogether, and that 20 percent of the American public favors summarily returning all immigrant arrivals during the past five years to their countries of origin. According to Dan Stein, executive director of the Federation for American Immigration Reform (FAIR), Americans generally are against immigration, if only for the reason that they believe it to be needless. Advocates of continuing, and even stepping up, immigration do not deny that public sentiment is opposed to them and to their cause. Immigration, Ben Wattenberg concedes, "has never been popular. One gets the feeling that when the folks on the Mayflower went out to watch the next boats come in, they muttered to one another, 'There goes the neighborhood.'" A survey by Rita Simon, wife of the noted immigrationist Julian Simon, of essays and articles printed by leading journals and newspapers from the middle of the nineteenth century to the present day comes to the same conclusion. In respect of immigration, public enthusiasm has always been limited to the fervor that inspired a line of graffiti observed a few years ago on the wall of a men's room in a café in a small coastal town in northern California: "Another day, another 5,000 aliens." Nor do the immigrationists, finally, deny that the United States has no *need* of immigration, Simon having himself acknowledged, "I don't claim that it is necessary; we can live quite nicely without it."

When one considers the existence of massive public dissatisfaction with current immigration policy, it seems reasonable to suggest that the real issue is, or ought to be, not whether immigration is beneficial to America or whether it is harmful, but rather if Americans want continued immigration at all. Under democratic governance it should be sufficient for *vox populi* to deliver a consensus, without it being required to formulate a rationale for that consensus. Since public opinion indicates near-unanimity on the question of immigration to a degree that is rarely achieved on matters of fundamental national importance, politicians and so-called opinion makers might well be expected to seek refuge in consensus as an excuse to avoid a debate that is inherently distasteful to them. Instead, they have not only encouraged public debate, they have made it inevitable by insisting, in effect, that mere *preference,* however widespread and deep-seated, is insufficient ground on which to base immigration policy, which can only be fairly and properly determined by the construction of a systematic intellectual and moral rationale. Their insistence is a further means of laying the weight of debate upon the restrictionists, as Fairchild observed their counterparts doing nearly a century ago.

The immigrationists would justify the demand for an intellectually developed case against immigration by arguing that because moral obligation, and not the national interest, is ultimately at issue, the claim that we do not need what we do not need is morally inadequate, and that any risk incurred by maintaining America's identity as a nation of immigration is simply inescapable. Apparently, they failed to consider the likely result of forcing the debate, which has been to cause their opponents to renovate and refine the arguments made by their predecessors in the early decades of this century, and even to discover and develop a few new-sounding ones. (Here, no doubt, is the explanation why the great majority of books and serious essays relating to immigration and published in the past couple of decades have been the work of anti-immigrationists, while the defenders of immigration have mostly restricted themselves to brief polemical pieces such as newspaper columns and articles in the popular magazines.) In this way, the unnecessary debate has become the useful debate, though—for the time being at least—only at its outer fringe. "Since World War I, the American government has relentlessly rationalized the processes of governance: we live in an era of scientific management. What has been lost in this rationalization is any deliberation over the ends of society, the collective goals that weld a diverse people into a culture." Oelschlaeger was writing in reference to our national shortcomings in respect of environmental policy, but his remark is applicable to the weaknesses of our immigration policy as well. Now that the immigrationists have challenged the restrictionists to produce an intellectually rigorous defense of their position, they may be compelled to do likewise on their own behalf, and so eventually those weaknesses may be reduced as the result of forthright, intelligent, and—above all—conscientious debate. As Governor Lamm and Gary Imhoff remind us, American society has often been advanced by the raising of painful and even heretical issues, while John Ney, in a pamphlet issued by the American Immigration Control Foundation, suggests that the immigration debate of today may prove as decisive as was the sectional one of the first half of the nineteenth century. "The Civil War was fought only after a great deal of soul-searching on both sides; for twenty years, from 1840 until 1860, compromise after compromise was proposed to avoid it. The immigration dilemma may, in the future, show increasing similarities if not a precise analogy. Perhaps the most profound issue in the Civil War was the future of the United States." Professor Nathan Glazer, in the mid-1980s, predicted that legislation pertaining to America's immigration crisis will continue to be introduced in Congress for the next thirty years. And as long as the legislation continues, so of course will the debate.

The immigration question, Michael S. Teitelbaum has said, is "a contest of 'right' versus 'right,' and always has been." In a certain sense he is correct, and it is a feeling for the elements of rightness on both sides that has led many liberals and conservatives into what Peter Skerry—a prolific writer whose subject is the Mexican-American community—calls "a conspiracy of silence" regarding immigration. Cutting across party and ideological lines, the issue creates discord in every camp; more discomforting still, the notion of "'right' versus 'right'" instills in their most honest spokesmen the nagging suspicion that—just possibly—they could be wrong. Albert Bigelow Paine's "The Development of a Moral Thought," a sequence of photographs of Mark Twain seated in a rocking chair on the porch of his last home in Redding, Connecticut, with handwritten captions inscribed by the subject, depicts the changing demeanor of the novelist as he wrestles with the question, "*Shall* I learn to be good? . . . I will sit here and think it over." This dilemma, which the creator of Tom Sawyer and Huckleberry Finn learned to exploit as the fundamental theme of his best work (frequently with ironic and often bitter results), is peculiarly American in its conception of goodness as essentially behavioral as opposed to metaphysical. An opposing school in American letters, exemplified by Nathaniel Hawthorne, Edgar Allan Poe, William Faulkner, Flannery O'Connor, and Walker Percy, substitutes good and evil for goodness and badness, order and chaos for right and wrong, but it is the lesser tradition in this country. "[U]ncontrolled immigration is an impossibility," Arthur M. Schlesinger Jr. says, but, "No one wants to be a Know-Nothing." That is the real American dilemma. It was also the foremost obstacle confronted by John H. Tanton and Roger Connor when, in 1979, they established FAIR for the primary purpose, as Tanton later wrote, of making immigration "a legitimate topic of discussion among thoughtful people."

Roy L. Garis, a prominent historian of immigration who was active in the restrictionist cause early in this century, published his book *Immigration Restriction* in 1927, when the national quota system was being instituted and refined by a series of congressional acts. "The amazing thing about the immigration problem," Garis wrote, "is the likeness of the arguments of one generation to the contentions of another. The points of view and prejudices of many sons are like unto their fathers'. Here, as in other enduring issues, there seems to be no new thing under the sun. How important, then, is the task of every citizen to think through the immigration question for himself, to free himself from bias, to seek only the truth!" Garis's observation regarding the continuity of the immigration debate from 1609 to 1927 holds equally for the period between 1927 and the present, especially the last decade, as the restrictionists have been pressed to reinvent not just the wheel but the entire wagon, which by now has become a well-appointed carriage. Additionally, many of the involved interest groups are the same, though their influence in some instances has waxed or waned, and some of them have switched sides. Also, several new ones have added themselves, most prominently those representing populational and environmental concerns. For these last, immigration restriction is not a reactionary but rather a progressive cause as, conversely, organized labor early in the twentieth century saw anti-immigrationism as a progressive program, whose purpose was to prevent strikebreaking by employers with plenty of immigrant workmen available to them.

In the 1990s, the immigrationist coalition includes the national Democratic Party and the establishment wing of the Republican one; the business and agricultural lobbies (largely Republican); the ethnic organizations (mostly Democratic) and refugee agencies; the urban Democratic machines; welfare agencies and others serving the needs of immigrants (legal and illegal); most of the establishment and business press and all of the major television networks; numerous columnists; the academy; the federal bureaucracy and many of the state and local bureaucracies; the liberal, radical, neoconservative, and libertarian journals of opinion; and the bureaucratic superstructure of organized religion. It is opposed by a slowly coalescing force comprising the Republican Party's traditionalist wing, organized labor, assorted taxpayers' and citizens' groups, some state and municipal governments, an increasingly alienated electorate in those states most affected by immigration, population-control groups and an increasing number of environmentalists, a growing body of economists who have become convinced that immigration has damaging effects on the American economy and on the American labor force, a respectable assortment of nationally syndicated columnists, liberal and conservative, and a few journals of opinion, almost all of them traditionally conservative in their views. The development of these motley opposing forces, perhaps unprecedented in American history, accurately suggests both the complexity of the immigration problem and the various interests entwined with it. It also suggests that Garis's admonition that every citizen think through the immigration question for himself, free of bias and seeking only truth, has not been heeded by a later generation. Never pity your work, a wise author once said. And don't get in bed with your opinions, either.

If the Democratic and Republican parties concurred on every issue of paramount importance to the extent that they are in agreement on immigration, the United States would have an overtly one-party system of government, instead of the present covert one. While some individual party politicians—for example, Governor Pete Wilson of California and the state's two Democratic senators, Barbara Boxer and Dianne Feinstein—reacting pragmatically to local and regional pressures and conditions do advocate restricting immigration, particularly of the illegal variety, Democratic and Republican officeholders collectively refuse to criticize current immigration policy and, when pressed, actually defend it. Many of them—Jack Kemp, former Secretary of Housing and Urban Development, and his Democratic successor, Henry Cisneros; Senator Phil Gramm, Representative Bill Richardson; former Secretary of Education William Bennett—extol without prompting or excuse the benefits of immigration to the United States, usually without drawing too fine a distinction between legal and illegal immigrants. As members of the party which in modern times has styled itself the champion of minorities and multiculturalism, as of all beneficiaries of the public welfare system, Democrats reflexively defend the indefinite extension—or expansion—of what they characterize as the hoary and hallowed tradition of "a nation of immigrants," while Republicans, since the Immigration and Nationality Act of 1965, have almost as reflexively refused to criticize it.

"I don't think you're going to find Republican leaders wanting to be pinned down on immigration," a Republican congressional staffer told Roy Beck, a reporter for the *Social Contract,* in 1994. "To stand against immigration is to confirm the worst things people think about Republicans." When a survey of 134,000 "grass-roots activists" conducted by the Republican National Committee in the fall of 1993 found party leaders and elected officials in agreement, five to one, that immigration levels are too high, the results considerably embarrassed the national party leadership. Of the ten top Republican contenders for the presidency, only two—Senate Minority Leader Robert Dole and Patrick J. Buchanan, the syndicated columnist and talk-show host—were prepared to express their satisfaction with the poll's findings. "While America remains the land of opportunity," Dole said, "it is not the land of unlimited opportunity for unlimited numbers of immigrants, both legal and illegal." Jack Kemp and Phil Gramm announced that the "apparent" grass-roots majority was "misled" on immigration and confided that they hoped to resist pressures for a reduction in immigration, and also to educate voters by convincing them of the benefits obtained by recent high quotas. "Immigration helps America," Kemp asserted. "You don't come all the way from Africa or Asia if you aren't willing to take risks. They are entrepreneurial. Immigrants bring a lot of skills and a work ethic that in many places has become passé. There is just a lot of work that would not get done were it not for immigrant Americans taking jobs that a lot of people won't take." Gramm concurred: "Not only is America a nation of immigrants, but new immigrants continue to build America and to expand its prosperity and freedom. We don't have room for people who want to live off the work of others. But I don't believe for a moment that new legal immigrants have been a burden to the economy. They have been a great boon." Both Kemp and Gramm explicitly rejected the proposition that continued high levels of immigration will in time overpopulate the United States. Kemp protested that he found it "unseemly of those on the Left and the Right who view America as a zero-sum game and that there's only so much to go around," adding that "When you take that to its conclusion, you end up with Bill Clinton and his world-population control policies". Gramm insisted, "We have room in America for people who are willing to work. I am not ready, nor will I ever be ready, to tear down the Statue of Liberty or close the door to America. . . . I've never found a necessity to have a correlation between population and government." Beck queried six Republican leaders—William Bennett, Dick Cheney, Dan Quayle, Pat Robertson, Bill Weld, and Pete Wilson—who told him personally or through intermediaries that they were insufficiently knowledgeable of the immigration issue to be able to comment on it. "This is not his issue," Bennett's spokeswoman explained. "He's not up to speed on it. It's not one he's studied and not one he ever speaks on. He has no expertise on it." Beck withdrew, seeming to have been too polite to remind her that her boss was at the time a senior editor for *National Review,* which had recently printed a great deal of copy on the subject of immigration. To date, the Republican National Committee has offered no analysis of immigration as a national issue, nor did its 1992 platform include mention of it.[2]

The evasiveness and disingenuousness evinced by the Republicans before the 1994 elections are matched by the Democrats' since the Republican landslide. While no Democratic politician enjoying national prominence equal to Kemp's or Bennett's had the temerity to denounce, as the two Republicans did, California's Proposition 187 shortly before election day (Bennett having apparently rectified his ignorance of immigration-related matters in the few months since his spokeswoman was interviewed by Beck), the party leadership was deeply affronted by the initiative. Nevertheless, with the exception of Jesse Jackson it kept its collective mouth shut as the Clinton administration, post-election, allowed Operation Gatekeeper—announced pre-election for the border sector south of San Diego—to lapse. Although Congress authorized several hundred new Border Patrol officers in the summer of 1994, their training and deployment were expected to take a year; in the interim, the patrol was compelled to meet emergencies in the most active sectors by shifting around its existing personnel. The White House ignored the recommendations made by its own Commission on Immigration, chaired by Barbara Jordan, and, abetted by the Justice Department, shelved what the *Los Angeles Times* had predicted would take shape as "a sweeping immigration reform proposal." Even so, the Clinton administration has stated plainly that its goal is to reduce only illegal immigration, while retaining high levels of the legal kind—a policy approved by Speaker of the House Newt Gingrich. The Contract with America, announced by the House Republicans after the November elections, included a commitment to cut welfare benefits to illegal immigrants, yet within weeks of his installment as Speaker Gingrich stated that he opposed translating Proposition 187 into federal law. Against this background, William Bennett denied that illegal immigration had become a national crisis.

The polls suggest that better-educated and wealthier Americans are more likely to look favorably upon immigration than their less-educated and less-affluent compatriots. Since better-educated and affluent Americans benefit more than other Americans from immigration, this finding seems reasonable enough. However, Julian Simon cites a poll, taken in 1986, according to which 48 percent of liberals, compared with 57 percent of conservatives and 45 percent of moderates, favored decreased immigration. That is not a broad spread of opinion. Apparently, while the gulf between restrictionists and immigrationists tends to run deep, it does not stretch very wide. Moreover, as a survey of the public prints shows, immigration as an issue is more ideologically divisive than it is politically. That conservatives are nearly as likely to favor immigration as liberals, while liberal critics have contributed significantly to the argument for restriction, and libertarians, after advocating open borders for a generation or more, now begin to waver, indicates the extent to which an American political consensus persists, the many reports of its demise to the contrary. If so, the present stalemate on immigration is the result of differences in stress and emphasis regarding the component parts of the consensus, immigration being in reality not a single issue but a congeries of subordinate ones, including nationalism and national sovereignty, free trade, freedom of movement, economic freedom and economic growth, democratism, and human rights, to name some of them. What these issues have in common is an intimate relationship to the question of the legitimacy of the modern nation-state, which is a construct of them all, and publicly defended by mainstream liberals and conservatives alike. Thus the nation-state, in the context of the immigration debate, is comparable to the proverbial elephant perceived by blind men for whom each part is a synecdoche for the whole. An excellent illustration of the adaptability of the consensus is provided by

National Review, the conservative journal of opinion founded by William F. Buckley Jr. in 1955. As late as 1968 Buckley himself in his syndicated newspaper column criticized immigration as an unnecessary risk that no other Western nation was willing to tolerate, yet his magazine's editorial policy, during the 1970s and '80s, was to avoid the subject of immigration altogether while managing to convey the impression that the editors considered immigration to be rather a good thing. Early in the 1990s the magazine's new editor, John O'Sullivan, himself a British citizen, broke out of this policy of benign neglect when he commissioned Peter Brimelow of *Forbes* to write several articles advocating drastic restrictions on immigration, and committed the editorial pages to an uncompromisingly restrictionist line. This *volte-face* was criticized by certain of O'Sullivan's conservative friends and allies, and applauded by others of them. But what was most notable was not the change in editorial policy *per se,* but the fact that the character of the magazine was in no way changed by it. Following its dramatic conversion on one of the most crucial and divisive issues of the day, *National Review* was not more conservative than previously, nor was it more liberal, and certainly it was as nationalist, capitalist, and Christian as ever.

The question arises, If immigration is ultimately referable to a solid national consensus, and therefore an issue on which all Americans of goodwill ought to be able to agree to disagree, why is the debate surrounding it so utterly nasty, filled with anger, bitterness, and contempt on both sides? One answer is that the participants are involved fundamentally in an argument with themselves, or rather with parts of themselves, and that if one part wins, the opposite one loses, so that there is no peace of mind or of conscience to be had in either event. Though immigration is essentially a moral question, the morality of its possible resolutions is not self-evident, and the consensus—based as I have said on the at least professed mainstream acceptance of the legitimacy of the modern nation-state—offers what appear to be equally valid arguments for immigration, and against it. No morally scrupulous person, therefore, can muster absolute moral confidence in his own disposition of the matter, and nagging doubts and uncertainties lead him easily to lay down his conclusions with a trowel, as well as to truculence and impatience with conclusions different from his own. A second answer is that the immigration issue has finally to do with the identity of the American nation, and thus, in small, with the identity of every American. Immigration, at both the national and the individual level, is a gigantic, unsightly, confusing, and infuriating blot, a kind of national Rorschach test. Identity, where both nations and individuals are concerned, involves components of race, ethnicity, religion, language, and culture— inflammatory elements in the contemporary world, all of them entwined with the strongest hostilities, insecurities, and resentments operating at the deepest emotional and sublogical levels. If immigration is a sword cutting across ideological and political affiliations, that is because people of every ideological stripe and political affinity are susceptible to the emotions provoked by the immigration debate, which is finally a personal quarrel masquerading as a political, economic, or humanitarian one. Greatest among those emotions is resentment which, besides leading to argument *ad hominem,* compounds the natural tendency of public debate to disguise private interest as concern for the public good: capitalists eager for cheap labor, more consumers, and short-term profit citing Adam Smith, chapter and verse, on behalf of more immigration; politicians hungry for added supplies of naive and manipulable voters speaking magnanimously of "a nation of immigrants" and of "compassion"; ethnic "leaders" covering their quest for power by denunciations of "racist" immigration policies; charity cut away from the root of charity, abstracted, and transformed into a variety of dramatic roles assumed by the charitable, some of whom know how to make it pay. In the course of the immigration debate, logic—the logic of politics, of economics, of charity—is endlessly stretched by the debaters to span chasms of hypocrisy, up to and including the breaking point.

The fight over immigration is almost infinitely complicated by its being not a battle between two sides but rather among many camps having too much in common, instead of too little: too many areas of overlapping agreement in addition to their numerous differences. The immigration debate is embedded in a matrix that most American commentators accept, and whenever anyone pulls up a single plant by the roots, he pulls up the garden along with it. Liberals hear liberals attack immigration, and call it treason; conservatives read conservatives defending it, and see treachery. Nearly everyone recognizes immigration as a moral dilemma, too present to be ignored, too significant to be fudged, yet because it *is* an issue of moral as well as of practical complexity, too many people, having allowed themselves to become paralyzed morally and therefore intellectually, fudge it anyway. Aware that no satisfactory solution to the broader immigration impasse exists, they hold stubbornly to their own small piece of it, against all comers. So far, the result is that little has been done about immigration policy; yet having no policy is a policy in itself, as a number of observers have remarked. Immigration is a crisis, both chronic and now acute, that must be resolved. But it cannot be resolved by slogans, by emotionalism, by moralism, or—especially—by a moral perfectionism that insists that, unless the resolution is morally irreproachable in every detail, we are not justified in applying it. Paralysis of policy will be overcome only by confronting moral paralysis, and moral freeze by logical analysis enlightened by common sense. To that end, a good first step is the reassessment of the myth of the United States as "a nation of immigrants": how that myth was developed, and by whom; whether it accurately describes our national past; and whether it serves as an appropriate template for our national future.

NOTES

1. John Ney, *Miami Today—The U.S. Tomorrow* (Monterey, Va.: American Immigration Control Foundation, 1982), p. 37.
2. Roy Beck, "Right of Silence?" *National Review,* 11 July 1994, pp. 27–35.

In addition to the sources cited above, works consulted in the preparation of this section include Henry Pratt Fairchild, *Immigration: A World Movement and Its American Significance* (New York: Macmillan, 1913); Roy Lawrence Garis, *Immigration Restriction* (New York: Macmillan, 1927); Nathan Glazer, ed., *Clamor at the Gates*: *The New American Immigration* (San Francisco: Institute for Contemporary Studies, 1985); George F. Kennan, *Around the Cragged Hill: A Personal and Political Philosophy* (New York: Norton, 1993); Richard D. Lamm and Gary Imhoff, *The Immigration Time Bomb: The Fragmenting of America* (New York: Dutton, 1985); Arthur M. Schlesinger Jr., *The Disuniting of America: Reflections on a Multicultural Society* (New York: Norton, 1992); Rita J. Simon and Susan Alexander, *The Ambivalent Welcome: Print Media, Public Opinion and Immigration* (Westport, Conn.: Praeger, 1993); and Ben J. Wattenberg, *The First Universal Nation: Leading Indicators and Ideas about the Surge of America in the 1990s* (New York: The Free Press, 1991).

II

FROM MYTH TO
MYSTIQUE

WHILE LITTLE HAS BEEN ADDED TO THE IMMIGRATION debate since the seventeenth century, and still less subtracted, what *is* new since World War II is the tone, as distinct from the content, of the argument, whose sentimental and practical nature has been replaced in the past half-century by an increasingly ideological one. "Government policy toward immigrants seems to have been more positive than public opinion. This disjunction has existed as far back as records exist, not only in the polls era but also in earlier times. . . ." Julian Simon for once has committed an understatement, the contrast between public and official opinion regarding immigration being nothing less than tremendous. Since the American people have historically opposed immigration, and since the Founding Fathers, as suggested by their more candid remarks on the subject, opposed it also, it seems fair to conclude that a split developed in American history—probably beginning after the Civil War—between the people themselves and their elected leaders. Fairchild makes plain that immigration, rather than being America's oldest tradition, is simply its most longstanding unresolved problem, addressed only in times of crisis and ignored in the intervals between them. How, and when, did immigrationism become the superego of the American conscience, and immigration itself advance from toleration to myth, from myth to mystique? My own understanding is that the immigration myth developed concurrently with American pride and power, from republican self-consciousness to imperial self-celebration. Its fortunes have tended to rise with America's imperialist ambitions, and to decline, periodically, as these lapsed. Four main currents have nourished immigrationist thought over the past two centuries: patriotic self-congratulation, French radicalism, imperialism, and—finally—globalism. To the extent that the current controversy is something new and fresh under the sun, it is because immigration is starting to be challenged by the more sophisticated arguments of what Otis Graham calls the New Reformists, liberal and conservative, even as a coalition of old enemies from the Right, the Left, and the New Left attacks the theoretical assumptions on which the case for empire, the New World Order, and what Clare Booth Luce called "globaloney" rests. Governor Lamm is wrong to complain that the American people remain "hampered" by immigrationism, since it is not they but their leaders who have succumbed to a myth of their own fabrication. The following pages attempt to trace the growth of this myth, which offers egocentricity as largeheartedness, disguises hubris as humility, and—to paraphrase Chesterton—threatens the loss of the best things in victory, rather than in defeat.

"[I]N THE BEGINNING," SAID JOHN LOCKE, "ALL THE WORLD was America." And in the first century of the British colonization of America, convicts, offered a choice between penal servitude on the colonial plantations and execution, often chose to be hanged.

The history of immigration to the colonies of North America, and later to the United States, may conveniently be divided into eight periods. The first begins with the settlement of the North American colonies by the English, the Spanish, the French, and other Europeans and extends to 1783, by which time, Professor R. Mayo Smith (professor of political economy and social science at Columbia University) wrote some generations ago, "the state was established, and any further additions to the population had little influence in changing its form or the language and customs of the people." The second period, from 1783 to 1820, was one of slight immigration when an average of ten thousand people arrived annually in the United States. The third, 1820 to 1860, was an era of heavy immigration, mostly Catholics from Ireland and Germany. In the late 1820s the federal government began to compile statistics relating to immigration, and by the 1850s nativism had become a powerful political movement. The sectional crisis, culminating in the War between the States, brought immigration to a temporary halt, but between 1865 and World War I vast numbers of immigrants arrived from central, eastern, and southern Europe, among them many Jews and still more Catholics; on the West Coast, the appearance of the Chinese, the Japanese, and other Orientals provoked the exclusionary movement. The period after the First World War commenced with the powerful restrictionist impulse that produced the national origins system as incorporated in the Quota Acts, which, fortified by the Great Depression, helped to keep immigration to the United States nearly nonexistent until shortly before the outbreak of war on the Continent, when a substantial number of refugees from the Third Reich were admitted. But in the two decades between the end of World War II and 1965, American immigration policy was subjected to drastic and finally revolutionary change, beginning with the refugee and displaced persons legislation and culminating in the Immigration and Nationality Act of 1965, which replaced the national origins system with a nondiscriminatory one that emphasized family reunification. The period from 1965 to 1990 witnessed the unforeseen consequences of the 1965 act, as tens of millions of immigrants poured into the United States from the countries of the Third World, and Congress and the executive branch attempted to grapple with the crisis in a politically acceptable way. Thus, in the eighth immigration era, the United States struggles to solve problems and difficulties, and reconcile concerns, that were familiar to our forebears for more than a century and a half before the American Revolution.

"Nation of immigrants" or not, the United States arose from, and was created by, a colonial population that grew over an elapsed time of nearly two centuries mostly by natural increase. In 1741 Benjamin Franklin estimated that the approximately one million colonials had been produced from less than 80,000 immigrants over a period of 120 years, during which the immigrant-native ratio was 1:12 (it was 1:4 between 1820 and 1900). Of these immigrants, the majority were English, while those who were not English were largely Scots-Irish, Swedes, Germans, and Dutch—all of whom, including the English, had constituted a single German race in the area surrounding the North Sea, as Fairchild remarked. The word "immigrants" designates people who move from the territory of one nation or state to that of another. And since the majority of Franklin's 80,000 "immigrants" were citizens of a single state migrating to its territorial dependencies, they were in truth not immigrants at all, but *colonists*. Both Fairchild and Thomas J. Curran, a modern historian, have described how the English colonists maintained a suspicious and hostile attitude toward the non-English immigrants, against whom they actively discriminated. They were, after all, not the eighteenth-century equivalent of the immigrant Sicilian peasantry of the 1890s or the Mexican *paisanos* of today, but the cultivated and sophisticated representatives of a world power, settled on the margin of a continental wilderness. Fairchild said it well. "[W]hile the colonies were undeveloped as regards their natural resources, they were highly developed in respect to their stage of civilization and their advancement in the arts. In this respect they were the peers of the most cultivated European states of the period."

Considering the preeminence accorded the economic argument on behalf of immigration in the past century and a half, one is startled to learn that it was absent entirely from the colonists' understanding of the subject. Fairchild believed that this, more than any other single thing, distinguished the debate in the colonial period from that of his own time, as indeed it differentiates it from the modern controversy. Apparently, colonial Americans found it impossible to conceive of a situation arising in boundless America in which superadded numbers from abroad circumscribed freedom and opportunity, and limited economic competition. Ethnic concerns, not economic ones, provided the basis for the restrictionist case in colonial times, which as it developed eventuated in such legislative enactments as head taxes, the bonding of ships' captains, and the barring of criminals, paupers, and other undesirables. Beyond ethnicity, the American colonists had a particular regard for the morals and mental stability of prospective immigrants as well as, especially, their religious affiliation. Baptismal water was thicker than blood, and colonial Americans despised an English Catholic equally with a Jew, a convict, or a pauper. In this way, "The English element . . . was sufficiently preeminent quickly to reduce all the other elements of its type. As a result of the character of the migration assimilation was easy, quick, and complete. While it was said that every language of Europe could be found in Pennsylvania, this diversity was short-lived."[1]

Immigrationists today are quick to remind us that many of the thirteen American colonies were established as idealistic enterprises intended to inspire the world (meaning, of course, the European world). Precisely because they *were* idealistic, earlier settlers of these colonies assumed the necessity for differentiating among those who wished to join them, on the basis both of their character and of the compatibility of their religious and political beliefs with the founding spirit of the community. Laws enacted to preserve that spirit significantly affected the colonies' development. According to Garis, "It was partly on account of these restrictions and prohibitions that the different colonies were enabled to maintain their characteristic existence and preserve their political and religious ideals." For example, in 1637, Massachusetts, relying upon the English code that criminalized dissent from the established religion, prohibited strangers (meaning non-Puritans) from settling within its boundaries without explicit permission from the authorities; the enabling law had its counterpart in every colony with the exception of Rhode Island. While the theological and ecclesiastical content of Protestantism was certainly of crucial concern for the American colonists, it represented for them as well a character type, whose qualities included intellectual independence, moral strength, and physical toughness.

Time and again, the colonists' right of restriction was challenged from across the Atlantic by the government in London. In 1717 Parliament declared its intention to transport convicted felons to Pennsylvania and dump them there. The colonial legislature, though not empowered to nullify this policy, declared its opposition to it nonetheless and went on to impose a fine of five pounds on all criminals imported into the colony, and to demand that ships' masters post bond for the good behavior of their more notorious passengers for the period of one year. Julian Simon is given to quoting the passage in the Declaration of Independence that accuses George III of preventing immigration to the colonies and the naturalization of foreigners. The fact is that Parliament for the most part entrusted matters of immigration and naturalization to the colonial legislatures, while its interventions were as often for the purpose of encouraging as of discouraging immigration to North America. In 1709 it naturalized refugees from the German Palatine and packed them off to New York; in 1740 it did the same with the Moravian Brethren. And in 1747 Parliament naturalized all foreign Protestants subject to its jurisdiction. It is true that it sought by the Stamp Act of 1765 to limit immigration to rebellious colonies, and that, eight years later, it prohibited it altogether—a measure intended to prevent an increase in the number of rebels against the king.

Clearly, the colonists were at least as ambivalent toward arrivals from overseas, whether these were immigrants or even colonists, as their nineteenth- and twentieth-century descendants were to be. Yet, by perseverance in regulating the quality and identity of those arrivals, the thirteen American colonies succeeded in preserving singly their individuality—Massachusetts *versus* Virginia, Virginia *versus* Maryland—while concurrently creating a collective entity that by the time of the Revolution was recognizable as the American people. Diverse though they were economically, culturally, and in their historical experiences, they shared a tradition based on Christian teaching, a British-Protestant inheritance, and a commitment to British liberties and constitutional self-government. Essentially a regional English Civil War, the American Revolution provided the colonies with a common experience that strengthened them, and was itself enhanced by the Herculean task of forging a constitution consonant with their particular habits, history, experience, and expectations.

Of the fifty-five members of the Constitutional Convention, eight were immigrants: four born in Ireland, two in England, one in Scotland, and one in the West Indies. Jefferson, Franklin, and John Adams favored a West Indian painter's schema for a Great Seal of the United States, which included a shield divided among six fields, each representing one of the six chief immigrant groups to the British colonies—the English, the Scots, the Irish, the French, the Germans, and the Dutch. Eventually Congress overruled the design, and replaced it with an alternative inspired by the motto *E pluribus unum,* signifying not the melding of ethnic and cultural groups but the unity to be achieved by the controlled exercise of the various state sovereignties.[2]

Thomas Paine, in his pamphlet *Common Sense,* published in 1776, expressed the desire that America should become "an amalgam of the people of the world." The historian John Lukacs, himself a refugee from Hungary, which he fled in 1946, is sensitive to the difference between being an American and being, say, a Frenchman or a German, recognizing that Americanness implies a universal identity as well as one that is national and parochial. Indeed, American nationalism has always had its doctrinaire and abstract elements, pointing beyond peculiarities of ancestry, language, territory, and history. Yet, as another (American-born) historian, Clyde Wilson, maintains, a significant aspect of the Constitutional settlement of 1787 was the implicit agreement that federal republican principles would not be overridden by nationalist doctrine. "Providence," John Jay wrote in *The Federalist* No. 2, "has been pleased to give us this one connected country to one united people—a people descended from the same ancestors, speaking the same language, professing the same religion, attached to the same principles of government, very similar in manners and customs." The founders never intended to fabricate an ideologically charged universalist dynamo of the sort that modern American politicians are comfortable with: an evangelical leviathan eager to make the world safe for democracy, and then pump democratist dogma into the cultural and political vacuums it has helped to create internationally. Nor, as Wilson says, did the American people of the founding era expect to become citizens of the world. If no one at the time appeared to notice the fact of their British Protestant culture, it was because that culture was taken entirely for granted.

John Randolph of Roanoke warned his countrymen against a literalist interpretation of the Declaration of Independence, especially in the conduct of foreign affairs. That warning has subsequently been repeated by many people, including John R. Commons, a reformer of the Progressive Era, a labor historian, and an advisor to the Immigration Restriction League. An advocate of Anglo-Saxon superiority, he was also one of the relatively few—fewer, at least, than has generally been assumed—real racists in the debate which preceded the Quota Acts. The opening chapter of his book *Races and Immigrants in America* (1916), while unabashed in its discussion of racial characteristics, includes the sensible observation that Jefferson and the other delegates from the American colonies, in endorsing the idea that all men are created equal, were not proposing a scientific view of human nature but working toward a practical political objective. "They desired to sustain before the world the cause of independence by such appeals as they thought would have effect...." The latitudinarianism that Randolph rejected was embraced later in the century by Abraham Lincoln, who in composing his address on the battlefield at Gettysburg discovered that the Declaration had dedicated the nation to a proposition. Despite there being no mention in that document of any such dedication, Lincoln's poetic reading raises the philosophical question of whether a nation can in fact be dedicated to a proposition of any sort, and whether, if it could, it ought to be. Is *any* nation justified in committing its citizens to anything beyond the welfare of their families and their country, their chosen or appointed work, and their God?

Quoting the founders on immigration has become an intellectual parlor game at which both sides can score points, though the advantage lies plainly with the restrictionists. While the architects of the new American nation can be cited on both sides of the issue, instances in which they contradict one another—and themselves—are mostly to be explained by the venerable distinction between men in power and men out of power, suggesting that while generosity in receiving immigrants indeed was imbued with a kind of republican idealism, especially after the French Revolution, immigration as a practical concern aroused suspicion and even hostility in statesmen of the early republic. "Why should the Palatine Boors," Franklin demanded in 1751 "be suffered to swarm into our settlements [in Pennsylvania] and, by herding together, establish their language and manners to the exclusion of ours? Why should Pennsylvania, founded by the English, become a colony of aliens who will shortly be so numerous as to Germanize us instead of our Anglifying them?" Thirty-six years later—the year of the Constitutional Convention—Franklin was still arguing for restriction, and against proposals that the federal government should attempt to lure immigrants with enticements. In 1782 (*Notes on Virginia*) Jefferson wrote that arrivals from monarchical countries would "bring with them the principles of the governments they leave, or if able to throw them off, it will be in exchange for an unbounded licentiousness, passing, as usual, from one extreme to the other." Elsewhere he declared, "I hope we may find some means in the future of shielding ourselves from foreign influence—political, commercial, or in whatever form attempted. I can scarcely withhold myself from joining in the wish of Silas Deane, that there were an ocean of fire between this and the old world." Control over immigration, Jefferson believed, ought to be entrusted to the separate states. Washington, when preparing to hand over his commission as commander in chief to Congress, addressed an Irish patriotic association by wishing Ireland well in its fight for freedom. He added, "The bosom of America is open to receive not only the Opulent and respectable Stranger, but the oppressed and persecuted of all Nations and Religions: whom we shall wellcome to a participation of all our rights and privileges, if by decency and propriety of conduct they appear to merit the enjoyment." And in a private letter written three years later he expressed the opinion that "our region is extensive, our plains are productive, and if they are cultivated with liberallity and good sense, we may be happy ourselves, and diffuse happiness to all who wish to participate." Nevertheless, as president, Washington refrained from indulging in displays of this form of *politesse*. In his first annual message to Congress he called for the rapid implementation of "a uniform rule for naturalization," and in 1794 he wrote John Adams that "My opinion with respect to immigration is, that except for useful mechanics and some particular description of men and professions, there is no use of encouragement." The first president's Thanksgiving Day Proclamation, in which he petitioned his fellow citizens "humbly and fervently to beseech the kind Author of these blessings . . . to render this country more and more a safe and propitious asylum for the unfortunate of other countries," suggests that he drew an early distinction between political and what we today term "economic" refugees.

John Adams agreed with Christopher Gadsden that "Foreign meddlers, as you properly call them, have a mysterious influence in this country," and prophesied that "Americans will find that their own experience will coincide with the experience of all other nations, and foreigners must be received with caution, or they will destroy all confidence in government." Hamilton, who given his preoccupation with financial centralization might have been expected to have broached an early version of the economic argument for immigration, thought that "The safety of a republic depends on the energy of a common national sentiment; on a uniformity of principles and habits; and on that love of country which will almost invariably be found to be closely connected with birth, education, and family.... The influx of foreigners must ... tend to produce a heterogeneous compound...." He warned of "foreign propensities" and the confounding of American public opinion, particularly where the disputes of foreign nations were concerned. While Madison remarked during the Constitutional Convention that those parts of America that had encouraged immigrants were the most advanced in population, in culture, and in the arts, he later urged that no alien should be accorded citizenship who "would [not] be a real addition to the wealth or strength of the United States." On the occasion of the expiration of the Alien and Sedition Acts, when the period of naturalization reverted from fifteen to four years, Thomas Jefferson, now president, demanded to know whether the country should "refuse to the unhappy fugitives from distress that hospitality which the savages of the wilderness extended to our fathers arriving in this land? Shall oppressed humanity find no asylum on this globe?" Since Jefferson in retirement criticized immigration in ways that were consonant with his prepresidential opinions, it seems fair to conclude that in this instance at least his liberality was being offered at the expense of the Federalist administration that had passed the acts, and that, like Washington, he was distinguishing between handsful of asylum seekers and boatloads of economic refugees. Unlike their late-twentieth-century successor who in accepting the Republican presidential nomination in 1980 described America as a "City upon a Hill" and a beacon to all mankind, neither Washington nor Jefferson regarded the Declaration of Independence as a blueprint for egalitarianism, universalism, and the Golden Door.[3]

In the early national period, from 1783 to 1820, when an average of ten thousand aliens arrived annually in the United States, immigration was scarcely a consuming issue. Still, opposition built steadily as first the municipalities and states, by honing their police powers, and next the federal government, by exercising its commercial ones, devised legislation to regulate the problems that immigration created. With the native population doubling every twenty-two years by unaided natural increase there was no need for importing workers and settlers; among those immigrants who came anyway, the most notable of them seemed to be paupers and criminals. The states took what measures they could to bar these, but in 1819 Congress asserted its interest in the immigration problem when it passed an act requiring that statistics be kept on passengers arriving in U.S. ports and restricting the number of immigrants inbound on a single vessel. The first federal act dealing with immigration, passed on March 2 of that year, was aimed only at easing the conditions of the immigrants' passage, but the next year witnessed the first compilation by the federal government of statistics relating to immigration, as well as the inauguration of a national immigration policy that over the course of the next century made immigration control increasingly a function of the federals, while evolving progressively refined criteria for the exclusion of unwanted aliens. Meanwhile, in the 1820s, immigrants were for the most part appreciated, if not actually welcomed. The great construction projects of the era were under weigh, and it seemed to many observers that without immigration—more than half of it from Ireland—the proliferating railroads and canals would have remained on the planning boards. Consequently, and in spite of the sufficiency of native stock, a certain openness developed toward able-bodied foreigners who came, worked hard, and behaved appropriately. "Thus," Henry Fairchild concluded, "the principle of an open door, and a welcome to the 'oppressed and downtrodden of all races,' became the established policy of the nation, and as decade succeeded decade acquired all the power and authority of tradition and usage." Already, however, an ideological component had intruded itself into the nascent immigrationist debate. The Federalists, maintaining the opposition to immigrants that had produced the Alien and Sedition Acts, continued to regard aliens as revolutionaries and conspiratorialists, and blamed them for their party's decline. But the Jeffersonian Democrats, who regarded immigration as a sign of national dynamism and prosperity, welcomed it also as a source of votes for the Democratic Party. Additionally, it was attractive to many of them as a fulfillment of the Jacobin notion of universal citizenship, which they had embraced with other principles of French republicanism.

But as early as the 1820s also, and to a much greater degree in the 1830s, a number of states and cities wrote laws restricting the introduction of paupers from abroad. One of these was Massachusetts, which passed a resolution calling upon Congress to curtail the arrival of foreign poor throughout the United States. In 1837 New York City complained that three-quarters of its municipal alms recipients were foreign nationals, in 1839 the city returned a boatload of indigents shipped by the city of Edinburgh from its poorhouse, and both the U.S. Senate and the House of Representatives considered the possibilities of deporting such immigrants. Yet the rise of the nativist movement was not a result of economic fears or grievances but the expression of cultural dislocations and resentments, though by the 1840s the argument had begun to be heard that immigrants were depressing wage scales by working harder and for less pay than the natives. Immigrant riots in New York, Boston, Philadelphia, Cincinnati, and other cities in the 1830s, and political attacks staged by them against the government; the proliferation of immigrant political organizations and the omnipresence of immigrants in municipal, state, and national elections; the dispute regarding Bible reading in the public schools and the insistence by Irish Catholics that public monies be directed to their parochial schools—all these were of incomparably greater consequence than comparative wages in a still wide-open society. "The root cause of xenophobia," according to Thomas Curran, "was the fear that the stranger threatened the culture of the native-born. . . . This nativist belief, like that of the Federalists, expressed opposition to a liberal, universalistic view of citizenship. The American xenophobes thought that they belonged to a national community and were intent on preserving the character and integrity of the community by retaining control of it." Curran's disparaging description of "xenophobes" as "frightened, unhappy people, seeking an answer to the cause of their dilemma" is compromised by his later admission that their diagnosis of social change in early-nineteenth-century America was accurate: the character and integrity of their community were indeed being threatened.[4]

The concern for social and cultural integrity was not restricted in this period to day laborers, mechanics, small tradesmen, and other supposedly frightened, unhappy, and confused ignoramuses. The *North American Review* in 1835 carried an article by a Mr. A. E. Everett who rehearsed many of the arguments against immigration that were to become familiar in his time, and to remain so down to our own. Among these were that the heterogeneity of the immigrants' backgrounds prevented their assimilation, that immigrants abused the American political system, and that they tended to establish foreign colonies in the nation's already crowded cities. Everett was skeptical of the claim that aliens were necessary to the health of the labor economy, and recommended that they be subjected to a far more discriminating standard of admittance. In the same year, Samuel B. Morse—the inventor, painter, and first president of the National Academy of Arts and Sciences—published *Immigrant Dangers to the Free Institutions of the United States through Foreign Immigration and the Present State of Naturalization Laws,* a book peppered with heated remarks directed at Catholic, especially Irish-Catholic, immigrants. Concurrently with the restrictionist case, the sentimentalist one (in Fairchild's phrase) was developed by the immigrationist camp. "[A]merica," a contributor to *De Bow's Review* wrote in 1855, "pre-eminently owes its growth and its prosperity to the amalgamation of foreign blood. To cut off, therefore, or to discourage its influx will be to check the current from which our very life is drawn. . . . Let us welcome the houseless and naked of every land to American shores; in the boundless forests of the north and the south there is room to make a home for them all. . . . Let us urge the oppressed and the down trodden of every name to the blessings of American freedom: the Star Spangled Banner is broad enough to cover, and the eagle that sits over it is strong enough to defend, them all." Early in the presidential campaign of 1840, the author of a pamphlet published by William Cullen Bryant's *New York Evening Post,* a Democratic paper, attacked Federalist-Whig nativism from the universalistic position when he confessed that "As a native American, and the son of native Americans . . . I blush with shame at the dishonor which is done to [the American political system] by those who, from the boasted rights and privileges of their birth, should be the first to do justice to its character, and to protect it from the degrading stigma of inhospitality." Such men, the writer believed, were in fact the worst and most unnatural aliens: "'aliens in their native land'—aliens in spirit to the institutions which they should proudly cherish as the most noblest inheritance of their birthright."

Twentieth-century scholars have considered a variety of causes for nativist activity before the Civil War and since. A list of these purported causes—bigotry, economic dislocation, social and psychological disorders, alienation, and loss of social status—includes everything but what the nativists themselves deplored. However, one modern historian, David Bennett, does do nativism the honor of meeting it on its own ground. Nativists, Bennett admits, did not invent the very real crisis in values they perceived objectively: Their mistake, rather, was to hold the alien population responsible for that crisis. It is difficult, however, to see how the aliens did *not* bear responsibility, save in the personal sense. Bennett himself suggests that the nativists feared Roman Catholicism for the authority held by the church in a country where no traditional institution, but the people only, enjoyed its like. James Lincoln Collier, another modern writer, describes in *The Rise of Selfishness in America* how immigration changed American culture, society, and politics in the nineteenth and early twentieth centuries by undermining, weakening, and finally destroying the rural Protestant culture of the early American republic, as the influence of the socially more relaxed Catholic and Jewish immigrants, settling into the largest cities, created a new urban America driven by individualism and hedonism and dedicated to mass culture. According to Bennett, the nativists believed their mission was "to save and cleanse the nation, to preserve for themselves that abstraction which some would later call the American dream." The significant word here is "later." Abstractions were of little interest to the nativists, whose concern was rather for the identifiable particularities, spiritual as well as physical, that distinguish one country from all other countries. Bennett is impressed by the degree to which the nativists identified themselves personally with the United States. Their partnership in the great nation gave them, he says, an assurance not only of uniqueness but of a superiority that must be lessened by their country's fall from perfection. "America," Bennett quotes a spokesman for the Know-Nothing Party as saying, "has done and is doing the world's work, establishing the only true principles of liberty the world has ever known. . . . The hand that guides this light is a divine one. . . . America has a mission to teach the world." The implication of the statement is that this early version of the "American dream" was solely for export, not for import. The sense of moral superiority the nativists allegedly claimed and that historians and politicians of the present day find offensive points at two possible conclusions: (1) "We are so superior that we should accept no one to our country," and (2) "We are superior enough that we must accept everyone, so that they may learn to become just like us." The nativists seem to have arrived at the first, possibly less arrogant, conclusion.

The nativist movement began in New York City when a nativist candidate from there ran for Congress in 1835, and spread as chapters of the Native American Association of the

United States formed across the country. Immigration restriction was a critical issue in the presidential election of 1844, when immigrant resentment of Henry Clay's running mate (Theodore Frelinghuysen, a Protestant professor of Christianity who during the course of the campaign drew attention to the extent of foreign political influence) helped to defeat Clay and elect James K. Polk. In 1852 the American (Know-Nothing) Party entered the political fray at the national level, with the original agendum of barring Catholics and foreigners from all public office and of fixing the residency requirement for naturalization at twenty-one years. The defeat of General Winfield Scott, who had been accused of nativism on the hustings, was widely attributed (whether fairly or not) to the unprecedented strength of the Irish and German immigrant, or "foreign," vote, which the politicians for the first time in an American presidential election had courted assiduously. In 1854 the Know-Nothings elected six state governors and seventy-five congressmen; two years later former President Millard W. Fillmore, who headed their ticket, received 25 percent of the vote. In the 1850s immigration as a political issue waxed steadily, partly in reaction to the Molly Maguires in the Pennsylvania coalfields and riots in New York City, whose mayor in 1855 compared immigrants to foreign invaders and demanded protection from the president of the United States. Further irritants included an influx of what one writer in the *United States Magazine and Democratic Review* called "European reformers" bringing with them "a host of extravagant notions of freedom" and "heads full of division of property. . . ." Resented also were attempts by foreign governments—like that of Württemberg in 1855—to dump portions of their unwanted populations on American soil, and then deny the right of the unwilling host country to return them (as Fidel Castro was to do in 1980). Like problems associated with railroads and the trusts, those resulting from immigration were growing too large for the state governments to manage, and by the late 1850s the issue was plainly coming to a head. The result might well have been something on the order of the restrictive legislation of seventy years later had not the immigration crisis been overwhelmed by the sectional one developing concurrently with it. The constitutional crisis distracted attention from immigration, which itself had implications for the states' rights controversy. Lawrence Fuchs believes that had it not been for slavery the Know-Nothing Party might have continued to increase in political influence. But the Know-Nothings were themselves divided on the Free Soil question, and the New England nativists—who opposed the slavocracy—were offended by the party's nomination of Fillmore, who as president had signed the Fugitive Slave Law. There intervened the Civil War, which permanently altered the ideological as well as the material condition of the United States.

The War between the States had two principal effects on immigration. The first was to commit the newly reunited nation to a program of unrestrained industrial development and urbanization, wholly congenial with—many said, and still say, dependent upon—a large foreign-born work force. The second was to replace the casual and unselfconscious nationalism of the early republican era with an instrumental nationalism better suited to an industrializing and modernizing nation with growing imperialist ambitions, and to substitute for the Federalist concept of citizenship a universalist one more consonant with that of many Jeffersonian Democrats.

Clyde Wilson has explained how the Civil War helped the "New England community" to succeed in a long-standing attempt to impose its ideals, blended of economic progressivism and transcendentalism, upon the rest of the country, and to establish them as the nation's primary goals. Antebellum, Wilson argues, nationalism was a "sentiment" expressible in a variety of acceptable ways. But the war itself was the crucible in which a new version of nationalism was produced. "It was during the Civil War, with the appeals to the Union as a mythical indissoluble bond, to unlimited exercise of power by the agents of a putative national majority, to loyalty oaths and the archetypal image of Uncle Sam, that American nationalism came into being." Part of the nationalist mythology forged during the war was what Wilson calls the "moral imperative," created by Jacobin notions of the equality of man and of universal citizenship, and embodied in the Fourteenth Amendment—an imperative that endowed the new American nationalism with its moral content, and also with the justification it needed for the program of centralization required to affirm that content. The result—a form of "universalized democracy" that is actually a uniquely American creation—was a construct developed from America's Anglo-Saxon inheritance.[5]

As is often the case with myths of the publicly created sort, this primitive version of the "first universal nation" was subject from its inception to a powerful popular undertow that continues to this day. By the late 1870s anti-immigrant feeling was very strong among the working classes, and in the following decade it spread more widely through American society. Immigrants to the United States between 1850 and 1920 in many ways resembled those arriving from 1965 to the present. They were preponderantly young males; the birthrate was higher among them than among the natives; their variety of languages was increasingly confused, and confusing; their alien appearance unsettled Americans; and they congregated in the large cities that grew ever more congested. They were, moreover, often resented as much by the second-generation immigrants as they were by old-stock Americans. In 1905 the mostly Jewish United Garment Workers of America passed a resolution, "RESOLVED: That we warn the poor of the earth against coming to America with false hopes. . . ," and asked that Congress declare a moratorium on immigration for a period of some years. America was sufficiently changed since the war that the complacency in regard to unlimited immigration—which Fairchild describes as endemic among the American public during the better part of the nineteenth century—was beginning to erode, as the immigrants skewed income distribution downward, exacerbated racial and ethnic tensions, created new interest groups seeking to influence foreign policy on behalf of their countries of origin, and displaced American blacks on the job market, as well as from the residential areas where they had succeeded in establishing themselves.

Opposition to contract labor increased, and so did complaints against the exploitation of immigrant labor. Since the

Supreme Court in 1876 had declared all state laws regulating immigration to be unconstitutional, the states had no recourse other than to demand that the federal government take over the job of regulation for itself. Observers speculated that, as one writer expressed it, "The conditions that have hitherto greatly favored immigration no longer exist in their full force," and that the market for agricultural labor in particular was overstocked. Against the popular grain, the developing immigrationist myth was augmented by the dedication of the Statue of Liberty in New York Harbor in 1886 (the "Colossus of Refuge," which John Lukacs credits with initiating a new phase in the "historical symbolization of the United States"), and by the Columbia Exposition in Chicago in 1893, where Chauncey M. Depew declared in his inaugural remarks that "This day belongs not to America but to the world. . . . We celebrate the emancipation of man."[6] On the occasion of the centennial of Washington's inaugural, Abraham Cahan, later to become editor of the *Jewish Daily Forward* and at the time resident in the United States for seven years, asked with unintended irony, "What would have been the despair of George Washington at the picture of squalor, penury and helplessness! How shocked would he have been to compare the country as it is today with what it was when he had first set her free to pursue her happiness!" To this question, the response of the majority of Americans might well have been that the picture of squalor could best have been avoided by substantially shutting off immigration to the United States. Christopher Lasch has suggested that the nativists' opposition to the "new immigration" of the 1880s and '90s was the result of their perception that the immigrants were unlikely ever to rise above the condition of wage laborers—a fact they were unable to square with the American dream as they understood it.[7]

"We are," Herman Melville wrote, "the heirs of all time, and with all nations we divide our inheritance." Walt Whitman called the United States "a teeming Nation of nations." And Ralph Waldo Emerson in 1844 described it as "the country of the Future, a heterogeneous population crowding on all ships from all corners of the world to the great gates of North America, and quickly contributing their private thought to the public opinion, their toll to the treasury, and their vote to the election." Toward the end of the century, however, another generation of writers and artists developed a differing view of American society in its relation to immigrants and immigration. "What is the future," William Dean Howells ruminated, "let the prophets say, anyone can see that something not quite agreeable is in the present; something that takes the wrong side, as by instinct, in politics; something that mainly helps to prop up tottering priestcraft among us; something that one thinks with dismay is destined to control so largely the civil and religious interests of the country." In fact, Howells the novelist found the immigrants to be fascinating, as one of what he considered to be two new and wholly American types, the other being the millionaire; later on in his career he volunteered his aid to struggling immigrant authors. But Henry Adams loathed New York City because, it was said, he thought that it gave more power to immigrant Jews than it did to himself, while Henry James deplored "that loud primary stage of alienism" that the city presented. "Let not the unwary . . . visit Ellis Island," he warned, while professing to long for "the luxury of some such close and sweet and *whole* national consciousness as that of the Switzer and the Scot." James concluded that there was no escape from the alien but into the past, and proceeded to effect that escape by emigrating to England—running the newsreel backward, as it were. And Owen Wister inscribed in his diary his hatred of the "alien vermin, that turn our cities to Babels and our citizenship to a hybrid farce . . . the invasion of the Hun, the Vandal, the Croat and all the rest of steerage."[8]

Ironically, the success of the "New England community" in establishing its brand of idealism as the standard of national idealism following the Civil War was in large measure responsible for the challenge in the early 1900s to the dominance of the "New England tradition," represented by an aristocracy that was Anglo-Saxon in its breeding and Anglophile in its loyalties.

Its leadership, typified by Henry Cabot Lodge, A. Lawrence Lowell, and Nicholas Murray Butler, opposed the admixture of alien habits and ideas with American culture; quite naturally it favored the restrictionist cause, seeing in immigration a cultural threat essentially similar to the danger that democratization presented to the Brahmin culture. As it also subscribed—however paradoxically—to the abstract concept of America as the unique embodiment of the democratic ideal, the New England aristocracy believed fervently in the necessity for forced assimilation, or, as it came to be called in the 1920s, "One Hundred Percent Americanism."[9]

The James brothers, though close in many of their opinions, disagreed in respect of the American city, which William enjoyed. John Dewey, Jane Addams, and Robert Park, the sociologist, as students and admirers of William James caught his enthusiasm by contagion and by example. It was, however, the metropolis, and not the forming megalopolis, that they appreciated. Addams and Park both were well-disposed toward the immigrants, but not for the reasons that immigrationists of that time praised them—that they worked hard, that the best of them were docile laborers and assimilable citizens. Addams, indeed, was more sympathetic to immigrants of the first generation than she was to their children and grandchildren since, a country girl herself, she approved of their rural and preindustrial virtues, which included unselfconsciousness, neighborliness, and generosity. Similarly, Park—a newspaperman turned academic who believed that "The social problem is fundamentally a city problem" for which the solution was the re-creation in an urban context of the functional equivalent of family, class, and tribe—observed that the immigrants who succeeded in transplanting the social structure of their European villages to urban America were also the ones who coped most effectively with its traumas. "[I]n some ways," Park suggested, "these communities in which our immigrants live their smaller lives may be regarded as models for our own." Thus Park and Addams, while sympathetic to the immigrants themselves, were implicitly critical of immigration, or at least of the effects it was having on American society. That their critical attitude could be extended beyond the immigration question to challenge the assumptions on which an increasingly centralized and nationalistic America was being created was demonstrated when Park's "new parochialism" found its echo in the "higher provincialism" of Josiah Royce. Royce, a professor of philosophy at Harvard University, had been born in California and raised as a pioneer child. He had no taste for cities and therefore no interest in decentralizing, but rather getting out of, them. Believing that an excessive mobility in modern times had led to "an excess of wandering strangers," Royce advocated a return to the province. "There must we flee from the stress of the now too vast and problematic life of the nation as a whole.... [N]ot in the sense of a cowardly and permanent retirement, but in the sense of a search for renewed strength, for a social inspiration, for the salvation of the individual from the overwhelming forces of consolidation. Freedom ... dwells now in the small social group, and has its securest home in the provincial life. The nation by itself, apart from the influence of the province, is in danger of becoming an incomprehensible monster, in whose presence the individual loses his right, his self-consciousness, and his dignity."[10]

An alternative to Royce's provincialism was Franz Boas's "enlargement of political units," which Boas believed to be the fundamental principle of the modern world. Boas shared the liberal conviction that human societies are characterized much more by the similarities than by the differences between them, and so he advocated the destruction of group sentiments and loyalties and the creation of a society based upon individual rights. For this reason, he welcomed the effects of immigration, and even mass migration, on America, where, he enthused, the urban masses had never known the "conservative influence of a home in which parents and children lived a common life," and hence had been spared the "unconscious control of traditional ideas." However, the truth of Lasch's observation that assimilation, like Israel Zangwill's melting pot, implies oblivion was not lost upon perceptive commentators of the period, and in 1915 Randolph Bourne published his famous essay, "Trans-National America," where, by arguing a position exactly the opposite of Boas's, he anticipated Horace Kallen's work in the 1920s on behalf of cultural pluralism, which in turn pointed the way toward the multiculturalism of the 1990s. Like Royce, Bourne feared a standardized monoculture and social conformity, not pluralism and chaos, since he was convinced that the destruction of "nationalistic cultures" was destined to produce "hordes of men without a spiritual country, cultural outlaws without taste, without standards but those of the mob ... flotsam and jetsam of American life, the downward undertow of our civilization with its leering cheapness and falseness of taste and spiritual outlook." Americanization, Bourne charged, was simply another word for that "tame flabbiness" that now passed for American life and culture.

In the great Progressive debate over immigration it was the traditionalists—or anyway the antimodernists—who argued for cultural pluralism, and the modernists—less traditionalist than establishmentarian—who insisted on Americanization, an opposition of parties and arguments that persists in the present time. But the concern of the cultural pluralists of the early twentieth century was to humanize modernity, not necessarily to alleviate the cultural domination of the Anglo-Saxon aristocracy. It was, in a way, an anticipation of the late-twentieth century call for an infusion of "new blood" into the United States, but in the more significant sense it was something else entirely. The pluralists of the Progressive Era were not demanding *immigration* as a means of promoting cultural diversity. They did indeed come close to saying that America now lacked an identifiable culture—the same argument, it might seem, that immigrationists and multiculturalists make today. But they were not claiming that a uniquely American culture *never existed,* rather that that culture was being smothered and expunged by the combined forces of centralization, urbanization, and homogenization—forces that to a very great extent had been created, and were being sustained, by immigration. The pluralism of Bourne, Royce, et al. was not some kind of futuristic vision, but implied the recovery of the rich particularism of the past, not least among them the American past.

Throughout most of the nineteenth century, immigration control was one of the few activities which a centralizing government growing rapidly in power and influence was in no hurry to assume, in spite of the concern with which the state governments and the American public in general viewed the problem of immigration. States frequently issued passports before 1840 and naturalization was effected by state rather than by federal judiciary courts, while U.S. immigration officials for decades did not distinguish between temporary visitors from abroad and foreigners whose intention was to settle in America. Congress did not pass the first comprehensive immigration bill until 1882. That law was followed by the Alien Contract Labor Act of 1885, which prohibited immigration by aliens subject to contract labor, was amended in 1887 and 1888, and was only laxly enforced. The most comprehensive legislation to date was enacted in 1891, but even so it was not until the following year that the Bureau of Immigration commenced detailed record keeping of immigrants entering the country through the seaports, and sixteen more years passed before the federal government, in 1908, did the same for those arriving across the land frontiers. The government rarely noted the immigrants' religion and did not record their race before 1899, although the act of 1893 sought to safeguard the public health from imported disease. Congress passed several more regulatory acts in the early 1900s, most refining the categories of those it deemed admissible, and housed the Immigration Commission within the Department of Labor, created in 1913. However, the history of Chinese and Japanese exclusion shows the executive and legislative branches of the United States government actively opposing the state governments, and also the will of the citizens of those states.

The Chinese first arrived in significant numbers on the West Coast during the California gold rush of the 1850s, and by the late '60s they were well enough established in the state to have provoked the hostility of the Californians, who resented them for lowering wages and discouraging—they alleged—white settlers from coming to the West Coast in search of jobs. After the U.S. Supreme Court found unconstitutional laws passed by the state legislature aimed directly at the Chinese immigrants (on the grounds that the prohibition and regulation of immigration were tantamount to the regulation of foreign commerce), California brought its case before Congress, which it besought to end immigration from China. In 1876 both the Republican and Democratic parties included exclusionist planks in their respective platforms, and a Special Joint Committee of the U.S. House and Senate issued a report endorsing California's complaint, adding that Chinese immigrants spread disease, engaged in prostitution, gambling, and drug-dealing, and did not assimilate. The committee recommended that the treaty with China be modified to include only commercial interests, while restricting immigration from Asia. "It is not believed," the report concluded, "that either of these measures would be looked upon with disfavor by the Chinese government. Whether it is so or not, a duty is owing to the Pacific states and territories, which are suffering under a terrible scourge, but are patiently waiting for relief from Congress."

When Congress dragged its feet, California in 1879 held a constitutional convention that reiterated its earlier complaints in a memorial, adding that "It would be disingenuous to attempt to conceal our amazement at the long delay of appropriate action by the National Government towards the prohibition of an immigration which is rapidly approaching the character of an Oriental invasion, and which threatens to supplant the Anglo-Saxon civilization on this Coast." In the same year, Congress finally acted by abrogating the Burlingame Treaty of 1868 with China, and by virtually shutting off immigration from that country. President Rutherford B. Hayes, arguing that Congress lacked the power to cancel a treaty, vetoed the bill. But he agreed to seek modification of the Burlingame Treaty, and to that end dispatched commissioners to China. Eventually the Chinese government agreed to a limitation, but not a prohibition, of Chinese immigration to the United States. On 6 May 1882, Congress, denying that either the state or the federal court system was empowered to naturalize these immigrants, placed a moratorium on the arrival of both skilled and unskilled Chinese. Six years later China protested the Chinese Labor Exclusion Act of 1888, but President Grover Cleveland signed the act and the Supreme Court upheld it: Further acts in 1892, 1902, and 1904 extended the duration of all exclusionary laws in respect of the Chinese. In this way the will of the people of California and of the state government was at least in some degree effected by the government in Washington, but with a gingerliness and a reluctance that were to become more pronounced in immigration crises from the end of the nineteenth to the conclusion of the twentieth century.

Indeed, no sooner had a kind of *modus vivendi* been arranged between the United States and China than troubles arose with immigration from Japan. By 1900 resentment was widespread against the Japanese, one thousand of whom per year had settled in the United States during the previous nine years, most of them in California. Citizens founded the Japanese and Korean Exclusion League in 1905, and in 1906 the San Francisco School Board decreed that all Japanese children residing in the city be sent to the Oriental school in Chinatown. This outraged the sensibilities of the Japanese government, and President Theodore Roosevelt publicly condemned the action—a curious example of the effect of global ambition on a man who was even then warning that the white race stood in danger of being outbred and overrun by the nonwhite ones. Roosevelt, however, did promise to halt immigration from Japan, and the board rescinded its resolution.

By the Gentlemen's Agreement of 1907–8, the Japanese agreed to limit passports to nonlabor emigrants departing for the United States. The agreement failed to placate California, which had hoped to see the Chinese exclusion laws applied as well to the Japanese immigrants. In 1913 the state legislature, by a law that was subsequently upheld by the Supreme Court, prohibited Japanese ownership of agricultural lands in the

state; seven years later a state ballot initiative widened the prohibition to include leases and all interests in real estate, and Arizona, Washington, and Texas followed suit. Despite all such
attempts to prevent their coming, however, the Japanese continued to increase in California, often arriving by way of Mexico and other Latin American countries. In an article, "The
Japanese Invasion," printed in the *Annals of the American Academy of Political Science* in 1921, John S. Chambers, controller of
the state of California, replied to criticism of California's exclusionary policies from at home as well as from abroad. "The
issue," he explained, "is a fundamental difference; not one of
superiority or inferiority. Granting equality, the standards of
the races are almost as opposite as the poles, and there is no possibility of a common trend ever being evolved. Assimilation is
impossible. . . . I wish to emphasize the fact that California is
not acting in a spirit of hatred, vindictiveness or retaliation. We
are actuated by the instinct of self-preservation. . . . For Japan
and the Japanese on their proper side of the Pacific we have
only good wishes; on this side, we cannot feel so because we
know that what they would consider their good would mean
our undoing."[11]

Most striking in the history of Chinese and Japanese exclusion is the resistance to it on the part of, foremostly, the executive branch of the federal government and, secondarily, the
legislative one, which moved to restrict immigration from
China and Japan only when its hand was forced by the affected
states. While deserving credit for its caution in regard to matters of constitutionality, the national government in these con-
troversies was constrained all too plainly by considerations
ulterior to the well-being of the American people, and in particular by the desire of the nation's leaders to cut a figure on the
international scene and to make America's will count everywhere in the world, at the expense if necessary of domestic
tranquility and republican virtue. In this it was abetted by other
interests and voices, among them the northeastern urban press,
which consistently and almost unanimously opposed exclusionary practices three thousand miles away in circumstances

largely unimaginable by Eastern critics. True, imperialist fervor in the 1890s and early 1900s was not restricted to the political and commercial elite, but was widespread among the citizenry as well. It was, however, essentially the creation of the elite class, beginning as a narrow intellectual movement among Progressive Republicans, which did its best to sustain the enthusiasm and was becoming adept moreover in the kind of disingenuousness endemic to political discourse in our own time. Roosevelt, seized with moral indignation when anti-Japanese measures in California were pending, admitted in his *Autobiography* that exclusion was "fundamentally a sound and proper attitude," though it needed to be tactfully accomplished. Believing that "we are becoming a polyglot boardinghouse," he saw that mass immigration from the more exotic regions of the Old World was certain to have a transforming effect on the United States; in fact, for Roosevelt immigration was one of the reasons why a "new nationalism" was necessary to replace the patriotism of a federal republic embracing a variety of regional loyalties. President Woodrow Wilson was more forthright when he stated in 1913 that "Invidious discrimination will inevitably draw in question the treaty obligations of the United States." His use of the pejorative adjective, however, fails to convey the fact that Wilson's own views on race were considerably less enlightened than those expressed by the aforementioned John S. Chambers, controller of the state of California.

After the turn of the century, opposition to immigration, which had surfaced at the popular level ten years before, was joined by the professional classes, which gave the movement an effectiveness it had previously lacked by developing and honing its arguments, and by giving it direction. Nineteen hundred and seven was the year in which immigration to the United States peaked at 1.3 million, a total which, in numbers of *legal* immigrants, has not since been surpassed. Hitherto the preeminent argument in favor of mass immigration had been that the economy of a growing, industrializing, and expanding nation required the importation of millions of people, but now the economic case was being reconsidered from a broader and more sophisticated perspective. In 1911, the Report of the U.S. Immigration Commission suggested that "The measure of the national, healthy development of a country is not the extent of its investment of capital, its output of products, or its exports and imports, unless there is a corresponding economic opportunity afforded to the citizen dependent upon employment for his material, mental, and moral development. . . . A slow expansion of industry which would permit the adaptation and assimilation of the incoming labor supply is preferable to a very rapid industrial expansion which results in immigration of laborers of low standards and efficiency, who imperil the American standards of wages and conditions of employment." A few years before, a U.S. commissioner of immigration had urged that Congress be empowered to establish an employment information bureau on Ellis Island to apprise immigrants of available jobs outside the increasingly impacted Northeast. His specific recommendation that they be diverted to the Southern states in particular was countered by the warning that immigrants arriving in Dixie would have the certain effect of driving the Negroes into the already congested cities of the region. Arizona passed a law requiring that every employer of more than five people hire a minimum of 80 percent "qualified electors," or native-born citizens, but the Supreme Court declared it unconstitutional in 1915. Frank Julian Warne, author of *The Immigrant Invasion* (1913), worried that "By continuing our present policy we choose that which is producing a plutocratic class of idle nobodies resting upon the industrial slavery of a great mass of ignorant and low standard of living toilers."

In the decades preceding the First World War, the growing consensus that immigration was a national problem requiring prompt and effective action expressed itself more in a concern for the quality of immigrants than for their numbers. Between 1896 and 1917, Congress passed four literacy test bills (1896, 1913, 1915, and 1917), all of them vetoed in turn by Presidents Cleveland, Taft, and Woodrow Wilson, who exercised the veto power twice and was overridden on the second occasion by

Congress, which went on to produce the Immigration Act of 1917. An obvious presidential consideration was the immigrant vote, though it is notable that a Republican president, as well as two Democratic ones, should have been constrained by it. But Wilson, who as president was to smash America's noninterventionist tradition forever by committing the country to the war in Europe, espoused the immigrationist position in the presidential race of 1912, as a campaign pamphlet from that year attests. The Democratic Party, Wilson wrote in an open letter to "a well-known foreign-born citizen of Connecticut," was committed to a liberal immigration policy by its origin, in opposition to the Alien and Sedition Acts by which the Federalist Party had attempted to halt the process of naturalization of foreigners. Three years later, Wilson in his first veto message sounded an ideological note that was to become institutionalized in American governmental parlance after World War II when he described the right of asylum as "a policy in which our people have conceived the very character of their Government to be expressed, the very mission and spirit of the Nation in respect of its relations to the peoples of the world outside their borders," and hazarded that the "children and compatriots" of earlier asylum seekers "must stand amazed to see the representatives of their Nation now resolved, *in the fullness of our national strength and at the maturity of our great institutions,* to risk turning such men from our shores without test of quality or purpose." (My emphasis.) As for the literacy test itself, Wilson argued that it represented neither a test of character nor ability but of opportunity, and that its chief intention was restriction rather than selection. He concluded his message with a piece of hypocritical sleight of hand that recalls H. L. Mencken's description of him as a "self-bamboozled Presbyterian" by remarking that if the American people truly wished to reverse the policy of "generations of Americans that have gone before them," he as their humble servant had no license to deny them. "But I do not believe that they have. I respectfully submit that no one can quote their mandate to that effect. Has any political party ever avowed a policy of restriction in this fundamental matter, gone to the country on it, and been commissioned to control its legislation. . . . I am not foolish enough to profess to know the wishes and ideals of America better than the body of her chosen representatives. [!] I only want instruction direct [!!] from those whose fortunes, with ours and all men's, are involved."

It is strange how societies, like individuals, can become agitated and excited by some problem or condition that appears to claim a significant part of their attention when, unrecognized by them, it has succeeded only in scratching the surface of their concern. A writer of the period, Julius Drachsler, perceptively described the attitude of Americans toward immigration before World War I as being one of "large generosity and of absentmindedness" induced by an "intense economic life" that succeeded in overriding fears of the immigrant hordes and of the foreign colonies growing unobtrusively but steadily at the centers of the great American cities. "Then, like a thunderbolt from a clear sky, came the great European War. . . ."[12]

In the crisis, the immigration problem reformulated itself as a loyalty problem, so many of the "new immigrants" having migrated either from the Central Powers or from those within their sphere of influence. As it happened, disloyalty to both America and the Allied effort were almost nonexistent, but the *apparat* created by the federal government to deal with "subversives," and outbreaks of local hysteria regarding supposed spies (which Washington did little or nothing to dampen), contributed directly to the Red Scare postwar, and to excesses perpetrated by Wilson's attorney general, A. Mitchell Palmer. The Palmer Raids, which eventuated in the deportation of the anarchists Emma Goldman and Alexander Berkman together with 247 other deportees on the U.S. transport ship *Buford,* raise doubts about the sincerity of the president's prewar statements regarding immigration. If Wilson actually believed his own words about deserving asylum seekers from abroad, then why was he so quick to assume their disloyalty to the United States and their continued fealty to the wicked countries from which they had managed to escape? As a candidate for presidential office in 1912, he had spoken—or rather written—warmly of how "America has enriched her genius, has made it various and universal, as she has renewed herself out of the ancient peoples from Norway to Italy and the rich lands of the Mediterranean who have made the literature and the history of the world." By the end of the war, he was only too happy to ship some of that genius back where it came from.

As the war receded in memory, the fear of alien subversion was rapidly replaced by a concern for national identity. The United States, which had entered the conflict as a bumptious Nemorino, emerged from it as a dour version of Doctor Dulcamara, a grimly moral presence in tails and a high hat: an international fixer not to be trifled with, and the world's number one creditor besides. The American nation, having achieved the status of a world power, had an important role to play, and, as Drachsler understood, in order to play that role effectively it needed to achieve unity within. The question was, Could the melting pot be relied upon to create that unity, or was some other means required? Frederick C. Howe, the commissioner of immigration, had predicted that five million Europeans would arrive after the war, inspired by the ideal of Americanism they had learned from the American troops. In the event, 805,228 aliens came to the United States in 1920, and the commissioner general expected two million per annum for the next several years. Nevertheless, American business interests clamored against what they perceived to be an immigration shortfall, protesting that they required as many as four million immigrants to operate their industries; the National Conference on Immigration, meeting in 1920, advocated that all restrictions be removed. In the 1920s the social sciences were at last coming into their own, having emerged from their primal academic slime onto the broad sunlit uplands of government bureaucracy. The promise that they held for a certain type of mind was powerfully expressed by Professor Drachsler, who foresaw "the possibility of so controlling the underlying social-psychic forces in American community life as to ensure the full unfolding of the creative powers of the immigrant populations. This involves nothing short of a conscious molding of the coming civilization of America. What more fascinating task can there be for a nation than to set about deliberately and planfully to create its own future character?" Seventy years before Ben Wattenberg put pen to paper, the age of "designer immigration" was announced. It was against this uncertain background that a series of legislative acts embodying the national origins quota system was drafted, debated, and passed.

For Roy Lawrence Garis, writing his history of immigration restriction in the 1920s, the national origins legislation was the product of nearly two hundred years' reflection and study on the part of the American people. Nor was the intense concern that produced the Quota Laws an ephemeral or episodic phenomenon, having been present at least since the 1880s and restrained only by a national government increasingly responsive to signals from foreign governments, and also to the ethnic voting blocs at home that were the products of immigration. Plainly, immigration restriction was by the early 1920s an idea whose time had come. "The United States of America," Albert Johnson, who served as chairman of the House Committee on Immigration and Naturalization Services, wrote, "a nation great in all things, is ours today. To whom will it belong tomorrow? . . . The United States is our land. If it was not the land of our fathers, at least it may be, and it should be, the land of our children. We intend to maintain it so. The day of unalloyed welcome to all people, the day of indiscriminate acceptance of all races, has definitely ended." Against such powerful national sentiment as this, the immigrationist argument that immigrants had played a large part in building the country could not prevail. President Coolidge, in signing the Quota Law of 1924, remarked that the necessity for a homogeneous culture—not the contribution of immigrants to the American economy— was the main issue at stake in the bill.

The Quota Laws imposed numerical limitations on immigration for the first time in American history, while retaining the qualitative ones. The first Quota Law, passed in 1921, was provisional. It restricted the number of immigrants annually from any country to 3 percent of the American population of the same nationality resident in the United States according to the census of 1910, and established a maximum general quota of 357,000 per annum. It was followed by the New Quota Law of 1924, which halved the annual total quota (164,447) and reduced immigration in any year to 2 percent of the derivative populations as recorded by the census of 1890. The 1924 law was to be altered in 1927 by a provision basing the apportionment on the distribution of national origins in 1920, as determined by intervening study, and mandating a fixed ceiling of 150,000 immigrants a year. However, owing to congressional wrangling the final quota figures were not permanently established until 1929, after which date they remained essentially intact until 1965, though modified somewhat by the McCarran-Walter Act of 1952 and, more substantially, by executive practice after World War II.

Nearly every writer on the subject of immigration policy since the Immigration Act of 1965—including restrictionists opposed to that policy down to the present time—has felt compelled to refer in passing to the intolerably "racist" basis on which the National Origins Quota System was founded. In fact, reference to the records and the literature relating to the debates that produced it reveals a marked sensitivity toward matters of racial and ethnic identity. In the protracted quarrel over which census, that of 1890, 1910, or 1920, should be established as the baseline—thus determining whether the intended legislation would favor the "new" or the "old" immigration— the argument that "nation" and "race" are not necessarily equivalent, and that politics frequently cuts across racial lines, recurs with frequency. Indeed, as Garis pointed out, "Grouping of immigrants by countries of origin does not give, or rather it conceals, information as to the racial elements making up our immigration tide." The intent of the legislators was to promote cultural, not racial, homogeneity in the United States by giving preference, say, to a British Jew over an Armenian Christian. The insistence that political boundaries are often artificial and arbitrary, inaccurately delineating nationalities, races, and ethnic groups, had particular cogency in the wake of President Wilson's Treaty of Versailles, and in the circumstances of the fiasco it had created in the central and eastern portions of the European subcontinent.

The charge of racialism, subsumed under accusations of discrimination, nevertheless did not account for all of these, since spokesmen for the immigrant groups did not wish their peoples abroad to be barred from the United States for reasons of nationality any more than of race. (Naturally they resented in a personal way the implication that they belonged to a type against which the nation required protection—which of course was the axiom from which the entire debate proceeded.) The "new" immigrants pressed for a bill based on the latest available census, arguing that to take any population other than the present one as the measure was clearly discriminatory. An answer to this argument was made by Representative William N. Vaile of Colorado when he addressed Congress in April 1924. "Now, it seems rather illogical for gentlemen who vaunt the assimilability and the work of alien groups in our population to claim that those who have been for the shortest time in the process of assimilation and in the work of the Republic should have greater or even equal consideration because of this very newness.... That people from southern and eastern Europe did not begin to come in large numbers until after 1890 certainly proves that those who came before them had built up a country desirable enough to attract these late comers. Shall the countries which furnished these earlier arrivals be discriminated against for the very reason, forsooth, that they are represented here by from 2 to 10 generations of American citizens, whereas the others are largely represented by people who have not been here long enough to become citizens? If there is a charge of 'discrimination,' the charge necessarily involves the idea that the proposed quota varies from some standard which is supposed to be not 'discriminatory.' What is that standard?"

The majority of the newspapers in the larger cities along the East Coast opposed the Quota Law of 1921. But the *New York Times,* published by Adolph Ochs, argued against making the census of 1910 the baseline for restriction, which an editorialist claimed would unfairly favor the new immigration at the expense of the old. Insisting that the point at issue was not the wishes of the potential immigrants but rather the right of the United States to say who should and who should not be admitted to the country, the writer added that the primary concern of Congress should be the good of America, not the welfare of foreigners overseas. "The great test," he concluded, "is assimilability. There is no question of 'superior' or 'inferior' races. . . . Certain groups not only do not fuse easily, but consistently endeavor to keep alive their racial distinctions when they settle among us." Three years later, the *Washington Post* in an editorial entitled "Speed Immigration Legislation" made substantially the same argument, taking to task the too many immigrants who had solidly resisted Americanization and even evinced resentment at the suggestion that they learn English.

Albert Johnson identified the parties opposed to the immigration legislation of 1924 as restrictionists who regarded it as overly lenient toward the immigrants; businessmen complaining of an insufficiency of native manual labor; exploiters of all immigrants save the criminal, the diseased, and the insane; people of "an international frame of mind"; settled immigrants wishing to be joined by their families, compatriots, and coreligionists; and advocates of designer immigration, interested in selecting for skills and for distribution. After several years of battle royal, the antirestrictionist coalition had been defeated by a plain though often inchoate sentiment that Kenneth L. Roberts, the popular novelist commissioned by Horace Lorimer to write a series of articles on immigration for the *Saturday Evening Post*, in his book *Why Europe Leaves Home* (1922) reduced to crystal clarity and a nonideological and unintellectualized simplicity. "All foreign countries develop laws which accrue to their own benefit and meet the peculiar needs of the different countries. For the United States to delay doing so is suicidal."

The tragedy of the Quota Laws was not that they offered too little, but rather that they came too late—after the horses had run into the barn. By the 1920s, even as immigration was being debated, the Old America—not to be confused with the One Hundred Percent Americanism of boosterism and other forms of Babbittry—had already been replaced by the New America, to which the Puritans as well as the immigrants contributed, in which all achieved a victory of sorts, and all, finally, sustained defeat.

At some unspecifiable point in the latter part of the nineteenth century, the Anglo-American aristocracy began to run out of social and intellectual vitality, and by the 1920s it had lost it almost entirely. The most trenchant chronicler of this decline was H. L. Mencken, whose savaging of Puritanism and the Brahmin culture of New England—indeed, of the Anglo-Saxon majority itself—has lately been eclipsed by his offhanded remarks about Negroes and Jews. Mencken understood from the start of his career that the cancer that had wasted the Puritan tradition was an abstracted idealism that expressed itself politically as a program to impose universalized democracy at home, and then to force it upon the rest of the world. He understood also that while the Puritan intellectual culture was beyond all repair and saving, the Puritan moral view—what George Will was to call "statecraft as soul-craft"—stood virtually unchallenged by all the major American political interests. Even Mencken, however, failed to see that the collapse of the culture of the Puritans—to which he himself contributed substantially—left a cultural vacuum with nothing around to fill it but the mass culture that prosperity, technological ingenuity, advertising, consumerism, and the resulting social and cultural homogenization were creating in the postwar era. And mass culture, as rapidly became apparent, had all kinds of affinities with the mass politics of universalized democracy, for which it prepared the way and to which it was very likely indispensable.

James Lincoln Collier has described how immigration before and after the Civil War undermined Anglo-Protestant cultural mores; how it proletarianized the American rural, bourgeois, and, finally, the upper classes; and how it directly transformed a variety of spontaneous folk cultures into a vast uniform "popular culture" created by deracinated hucksters who had never crossed the Hudson River. And after popular music and vaudeville came Hollywood, whose products John Lukacs aptly describes as having been "put together by people whose origins and backgrounds and aspirations were worlds apart from those of the older Anglo-Saxon Americans." Frank Lloyd Wright, an Old American who despised the modern American city, loathed as well what he termed "The Broadway Creed." "The Broadway Creed," he said, "has covered the country pretty much until it has Hollywood for its other end. . . . Selfishly bred, children of pleasure herding on hard, crowded pavements in congested urban areas, the breed naturally gets the worm's-eye view suited to the Cashandcarry mentality. In spite of the Immigration laws, it has grown up among us as the natural product of the melting pot." By the 1920s, Americans had already fallen into the habit of being entertained, rather than of entertaining themselves. Already they were jaded by the familiar, and accustomed to responding automatically and indiscriminately to novelties, among them hot dogs, spaghetti, pizza, and oriental food. "In these, as in many other instances, the adaptation of new tastes and habits by the native population came even more swiftly than the adaptations of American tastes and habits by the immigrants." As for those immigrants, they conformed to America *as they understood it:* becoming approximations of Americans, learning the modern conformities much more readily than they learned the traditions, and in this way contributing to the growth of the new statism that was emerging from older forms of American nationalism.[13]

Increasingly, the New Americanism demanded conformity rather than contact with tradition, and in the New America the most obvious, as well as the most pleasurable, means of conforming was to consume. Lukacs reminds us that "Americanism," and hence "Americanization," were progressive ideas at the beginning of the twentieth century; Christopher Lasch has explained the significance of consumption for nineteenth- and twentieth-century liberalism in its efforts to create the liberal secular state and to achieve never-ending prosperity without setback or respite. Since Adam Smith, consumption has been recognized as the means by which nations could break out of what had previously been accepted as the inevitable pattern of rise, decline, and fall, and achieve immortality by following a linear path eternally upward. In the context, it is interesting that Horace Kallen, the father of cultural pluralism, believed that human felicity and social stability rest on a consensus regarding the disagreeability of work and its socially peripheral function as the guarantor of consumption as "the chief end of social existence"; also that the New Deal economists Simon Patten and Rexford G. Tugwell both were consumerists.[14] Perhaps the economic argument for immigration is better stated in terms of increased consumption rather than of added production. However that may be, consumption *was* a principal means by which immigrants in the 1920s came to participate in the national life and became "Americanized." Unfortunately, it was also one of the less attractive forms of Americanism available for emulation. Maybe it was even the very worst.

Looking back on the Law of 1924 from the vantage of the 1950s, John Higham, the immigration historian, concluded that its effect had been to negate the influence of the foreign-born in American history. From 1930 to 1970, immigration to the United States averaged 185,000 per annum. With the onset of the Depression, immigration fell to nearly nothing; indeed, there may have been years in the early 1930s when it was exceeded by emigration, although the figures are difficult to prove, since the government—then as today—did not keep records pertaining to emigrants. And as immigration declined, so American nativist movements, including the Ku Klux Klan, declined also. According to John F. Kennedy, nativism "died when a genuine crisis, the depression, turned people's attention away from the phony issue of racism to the real problems facing the nation."[15] Of far greater importance than the Depression, however, was the obvious fact that, with immigration virtually shut off, Americans who opposed the arrival of immigrants to the United States had nothing further to complain of on that score. Sixty years later, restrictionists look back to the nearly two decades between 1924 and the early 1940s as one of several prolonged resting periods in American immigration history when the nation was permitted to catch its breath and concentrate on its digestion, like a great snake processing the goat it has engorged. Unfortunately, the story is not so simple as that. While it is certainly true that uninterrupted immigration works powerfully against assimilation, significant waves of immigrants, even those separated by wide troughs, appear to be the single best explanation for the difficulty the United States has had over the past century and a quarter in developing, solidifying, and maintaining its essential culture, inherited from its Anglo-Protestant heritage and modified significantly by the influence of the frontier, which Frederick Jackson Turner identified as the uniquely formative ingredient in the growth of the American character and of American institutions. While the influence of immigration had long been apparent to percipient observers including Professor Turner himself, who was a restrictionist, immigration's long-term effects were sufficiently subtle in their manifestations as to pass largely unnoticed in the 1930s—a decade in which the purveyors of the immigrationist myth did not rest, as the fiftieth anniversary of the Statue of Liberty showed.

In 1936 President Roosevelt was hard-pressed between the isolationist Right and the interventionist Left, in particular by groups demanding that he adopt a more generous policy in respect of European leftists and, especially, the German Jews. Thus his speech, delivered from the base of the statue, was carefully shaped to appeal to the interventionists, and calculated to snatch away the veils the Liberty League had draped about the shoulders of Miss Liberty by shrewd references to "freedom from regulation, from government intervention, and from the encroaching welfare state." "Perhaps," Roosevelt said, "Providence did prepare this American continent to be a place of the second chance. Certainly millions of men and women have made it that.... The immigrants brought to us strength and moral fiber developed in a civilization centuries old but fired anew by the dream of a better life in America.... They adopted this homeland because in this land they found a home in which the things they most desired could be theirs—freedom of opportunity, freedom of thought, freedom to worship God. Here they found life because here there was freedom to live." As the hundredth anniversary of the statue in 1986 was to be converted into a celebration of multiculturalism, so the fiftieth became a symbolic protest against Roosevelt's ostensible foreign policy, pointedly expressed by James Benet when he referred to "the particular liberty to which this statue is dedicated, the freedom of asylum. . . ." Benet was wrong, however. Frederick-August Bartholdi, the statue's creator, intended his work as a monument to the principles of republicanism and to the amity between the French and American nations, not to immigrants and immigrationism. Originally conceived as a symbol of "Liberty Enlightening the World," the Statue of Liberty was transformed into the "Mother of Exiles" by what Elizabeth Koed calls "a mere accident of propinquity" when, six years after its erection in New York Harbor, the federal government built an immigrant inspection station on nearby Ellis Island. The plaque inside the pedestal, embossed with Emma Lazarus's poem, was placed there in 1903, but the "huddled masses" to which the verse referred had at the time no correspondence in American law, since "refugee" was defined only after World War II, when it was applied to a person suffering not economic hardship but persecution by Communist government.[16]

The virtual halt in immigration before the Second World War, and the sense of relaxation that Americans consequently felt regarding one of the very few national problems that must have appeared actually to have been resolved during the 1930s, were likely responsible—more than the apparent assimilation of the last wave of immigrants to make it into the country before the act of 1924 took effect—for the absence of antialien hysteria, or even sentiment, during World War II. But the war itself, despite sealed national boundaries and the hazards of transoceanic passage, proved an impetus to pro-immigration legislation, chiefly as a result of the good feeling existing between the Allies in combat against the Axis Powers. Representative Walter Judd, a former missionary in China, Pearl S. Buck, and a number of other scholars and authors formed the Citizens Committee to Repeal Chinese Exclusion—chaired by Richard Walsh, editor of *Asia and the Americas*—which succeeded in having the Chinese Exclusion Acts expunged from the books, and an annual quota of 105 Chinese installed.

However, the great changes in immigration-related thought and policy occurred after the war. The racialism of the National Socialist Party in Germany had the effect of discrediting entirely theories of racial differences; a fact which, when combined with the onset of the Cold War and the separation of millions of families in Europe, shifted the debate from questions of ethnicity to political considerations and the desirability of family reunification. In addition, the perception increased among restrictionists that the paramount threat to American security was not racial but ideological: in David Bennett's phrase, one "emanating from the head and not the blood!" But the engine of immigration reform postwar was the Displaced Persons legislation, in which the Republican Party—increasingly tempted to internationalism by the Cold War, and also by the simple fact of America's military and economic power—concurred. Of course, dissenters stood up on both sides of the aisles. Senator Elmer Thomas, in an article printed in *Modern Industry* in 1947, advocated suspending immigration entirely for a period of five years as a protection for returning servicemen in their search for jobs and homes; he added that the United States, as only a comparatively new country with no frontiers left, needed to reconsider the wisdom of admitting aliens for settlement. Representative Ed Gossett chastised the Displaced Persons program as "one of the largest, best-paid lobbies in the city of Washington at this time. . . . They are backed up by a nationwide organization that has spent and is spending millions of dollars in propaganda." The DP camps, Gossett asserted, were filled with people who had "displaced themselves," and should have been abolished long before. But Congress after 1945 passed a stream of refugee legislation, including the Displaced Persons Act in 1948, signaling that Republicans and Democrats, hardly differing in respect of immigration policy, deferred to the Truman administration. For what was only the second time in American politics, the executive and legislative branches were approaching agreement on the matter of immigration.

One writer has described the Displaced Persons Act as "a crack in the door" that eventually swung wide open to allow an emotional debate on American immigration policy that seventeen years later produced the Immigration Act of 1965.[17] The American public, expecting depression to follow upon war, saw no reason to alter the nation's immigration code, in particular the national origins plan on which the laws were based. Veterans groups and patriotic and ancestral organizations opposed the legislation, whose supporters included the Citizens Committee on Displaced Persons, largely a creation of the American Jewish Committee. President Truman in signing the act complained that it was "flagrantly discriminatory" against Jews and Catholics—a statement that spokesmen for the Roman Catholic Church denied. Public perception to the contrary, the majority of DPs were Gentiles, while later amendments included such groups as Polish veterans of the war stranded in Great Britain. In the words of the Displaced Persons Commission, "The DP Act of 1948 marked a turning point in American immigration policy, and in foreign policy. For the first time in this century, restrictive and exclusionary legislation was relaxed in order to facilitate the admission of refugees into [the] country." As David Reimers has noted, the claim by the DPC was wildly exaggerated. Nevertheless, the legislative battle that eventually produced the act of 1948 was an omen of things to come.

A proposal by Senator Chapman Revercomb the previous year urging a reconsideration of the immigration code led to the formation of a Senate subcommittee, chaired by Senator Pat McCarran, which produced the comprehensive report that was later embodied in the McCarran-Walter Act of 1952. The Senate Judiciary Committee's report described the national origins system as "a rational and logical method of numerically restricting immigration in such a manner as to best preserve the sociological and cultural balance in the population of the United States"; a characterization from which Senators Herbert Lehman of New York and Hubert Humphrey of Minnesota— joined by Representative Emanuel Celler of Brooklyn—sharply dissented, Lehman denouncing its philosophical basis as "strikingly similar to the basic racial philosophy espoused . . . in Nazi Germany a few years ago." In repealing all racial criteria as a test for citizenship, the sponsors of McCarran-Walter believed that they had answered complaints of scientific racialism, while retaining the culturally selective foundation of the national origins system. Working on the assumption that the United States no longer was a field for colonization, and therefore justified morally in exercising a greater selectivity than hitherto in receiving immigrants, they produced a bill which was, as the historian Robert Divine described it, "In essence an act of conservation rather than of intolerance." "[A] solution of the problems of Europe and Asia," Senator McCarran himself observed, "... will not come as we transplant these problems en masse to the United States of America." But President Truman, expressing moral outrage, vetoed the bill. The national origins scheme, he charged, was "absurd and cruel," an "outdated notion." Truman insisted that American immigration policy was vital to the continued growth and internal development of the United States, to its economic and social strength, and thus to the defense of the free world. "Our immigration policy is equally, if not more important to the conduct of our foreign relations and to our responsibilities for moral leadership in the struggle for world peace." The House overrode his veto by a vote of 278–113, and the Senate by 57–26.

But in vetoing McCarran-Walter, Truman had demanded a special Commission on Immigration which, oblivious to Congress's lack of enthusiasm, he appointed later in the year. In its report, issued the year after, the commission asserted that "the immigration law is an image in which other nations see us. It tells them how we really feel about them and their problems, and not how we say we do." Immigration quotas, the commissioners suggested, ought to be fixed not in accordance with American capacity and American needs, but with the desires and wants of the putative immigrants themselves! Their recommendation plainly was congruent with the president's message to Congress in March 1952, when he had suggested that the United States should strengthen the North Atlantic Community by accepting more refugees and relieving overpopulation in Europe. The *Saturday Evening Post,* which had pursued a strong restrictionist editorial policy from at least the 1920s, responded to the commission's report by remarking that "We cannot substantially relieve overpopulation and admit 150,000 people a year to the United States. Much as we might wish to do so for humanitarian reasons, we cannot destroy our immigration standards to take care of people who are surplus elsewhere."

Congress, in the debate on the Refugee Relief Act of 1953 and afterward, continued to resist attempts by political liberals and various ethnic, religious, and charitable organizations to abolish the national origins system and otherwise effect major changes in existing immigration law. But its efforts were substantially undercut by amendments to McCarran-Walter, added over the subsequent decade, that gave to the executive branch the means of circumventing its provisions by allowing the attorney general, through the parole authority, broad discretion in accepting entrants—mainly refugees—outside the quotas. In this manner Presidents Truman, Eisenhower, and Kennedy succeeded in defying the will of both Congress and the American public. As president, Eisenhower signed an amendment to the Immigration and Nationality Act authorizing an increase of 30,000 immigrant visas annually; the result was higher levels of immigration from non-Western countries than the nation had experienced since before the 1920s. "Perhaps," John Lukacs suggests, "it is not coincidental that in the same 1956 platform the foreign policy plank of that previously 'conservative' and 'isolationist' Republican Party called for nothing less than the 'establishment of American naval and air bases around the world.'" The youthful senator from Massachusetts, in a small book on immigration that he somehow found the time to write, explained how the government *had* to resort to "temporary expedients" to meet "emerging situations" that the "inflexibility" of the national origins plan left it otherwise incapable of handling. After becoming president, John Fitzgerald Kennedy found a means of evading that system by authorizing 18,000 alien relatives of recent immigrants to enter the United States outside the quotas legally allotted to their respective countries. The Kennedy administration, also without congressional approval, fixed quotas for the black nations of the West Indies that had lately been granted independence, slackened restrictions on immigrants suffering from a variety of noxious and infectious diseases, and devised more lenient indices for identifying economic refugees.

"Every step forward in immigration legislation since World War II bore the John F. Kennedy imprint: the Displaced Persons Act and the Refugee Relief Act, which he sponsored while in Congress; the 1957 bill to bring families together, which he led to passage in the Senate; and the comprehensive reform of our law which he recommended to Congress as President." The boast comes from the foreword, written by Robert F. Kennedy, to the posthumous edition of his brother's *A Nation of Immigrants,* the first edition of which, published by a noncommercial house, had scarcely been noticed when it appeared in 1958. Indeed, American immigration law was never far from John Kennedy's mind: As the scion of a proud but *arriviste* and even unsavory family which resented the Brahmin aristocracy's refusal to accept them at the value that they had assigned themselves, Kennedy may even be said to have been obsessed with it. According to people intimately acquainted with him, few subjects excited his resentful ire as that of immigration did. For Kennedy, the national origins system was a personal insult, an unwelcome reminder that for all of the Kennedy clan's pretension to a noble distinction, they were considered no more than shanty Irish bootleggers by the very people whom they wished most to impress. In addition to ethnicity the Kennedys' religion counted against them socially; a 350-year tradition of anti-Catholicism, unsurprising in a country founded and built by Protestants, further exacerbated the wrath of the first Roman Catholic president of the United States. While the Irish had been a significant presence in America since the 1700s, the case of the Kennedys (these particular Kennedys) goes to show how imperfectly the assimilation of the potato-famine immigrants, as measured by their resentment of the Anglo-Protestant majority, had proceeded since the middle of the nineteenth century. For John F. Kennedy, immigration reform was a club with which to beat down his own social insecurities, as well as the cause of them.

There is, of course, no trace of rage in the bland and characterless sentences comprising *A Nation of Immigrants,* nearly

every one of which encapsulates some fragment of the immigrationist myth devised and purveyed since before the First
World War by government officials and politicians of both parties. By the 1950s, this myth, having acquired a potent mystique, had swelled to encompass a myriad high-sounding
justifications for immigration on a large scale embracing every
imaginable consideration, from Armageddon (Prevention of)
to Zagreb, and thus offering Kennedy many polite and *faux*-
idealistic arguments upon which to draw. His argument was
unexceptionable, a distillation of the talk in congressional
cloakrooms and in the offices of special-interest groups. "The
use of a national origins system is without basis in either logic
or reason. It neither satisfies a national need nor accomplishes
an international purpose. In an age of interdependence among
nations such a system is an anachronism, for it discriminates
among applicants for admission into the United States on the
basis of accidental birth. . . . Immigration policy should be generous; it should be fair; it should be flexible. With such a policy
we can turn to the world, and to our own past, with clean hands
and a clean conscience. Such a policy would be but a reaffirma-
tion of old principles." Adolph Ochs and his editorial writers,
who had so sensibly defended the national origins plan at its
inception, could have rolled over in their graves.

President Kennedy made his work on *A Nation of Immigrants* the basis for the proposed immigration reforms that he
sent to Congress on 23 July 1963. The chief executive desired
three criteria for admission: skills, family reunification, and
priority in application. But he asked for no significant increase
in the numbers of immigrants admitted, merely a modest
increase from the present limit of 156,700 per annum.
(Kennedy did wish to allow in more Asians and West Indian
immigrants, and favored an expanded quota for mentally ill
persons.) At the time of his death revisions were already begun
on *A Nation of Immigrants;* following the assassination Robert
Kennedy undertook to complete the job and compose a foreword. "I know of no cause," he wrote, "which President
Kennedy championed more warmly than the improvement of
our immigration policies. . . . When President Kennedy sent

his historic message to Congress in 1963 calling for a complete revision of the immigration law, he decided it was also time to revise the book for use as a weapon of enlightenment in the coming legislative battle." The phrase "weapon of enlightenment" was especially well-chosen.

The Immigration and Nationality Act of 1965 is unquestionably John Kennedy's direct legacy, passed as a tribute to his memory. Published in 1964, the revised edition of the dead president's book was launched into a milieu which took the indefensibility of the national origins system for granted. In its review of *A Nation of Immigrants, Newsweek* remarked that it manifested "[s]ome of [Kennedy's] finest qualities," and referred to the abolition of the quotas as a litmus test of America's willingness to make amends for centuries of social and racial injustice. The *Saturday Evening Post,* which in the late '50s had anticipated many of the social, cultural, and environmental problems associated with immigration, in the fall of 1964 executed a *volte-face*—for which it offered no explanation—by printing excerpts from *A Nation of Immigrants* and by extending an editorial welcome "not only [to] the opulent and respectable stranger, but the oppressed and persecuted of all nations and religions; whom we should welcome to a participation in all our rights and privileges. . . ." "We are all," the editors added primly, "immigrants, except for the American Indian." Concurrently, the business and commercial press were predicting a labor shortage—"just as," Ira Mehlman of FAIR notes, "the front end of the great baby boom was entering the labor force." There was, in result, no more than feeble congressional opposition to the bill that became the Immigration and Nationality Act of 1965, and that mainly from southern Democrats and various conservative groups of low visibility. In Lawrence Auster's wry understatement, "The lack of a strong opposition resulted in a lack of serious debate."

As chairman of the Senate subcommittee hearings and floor manager of the bill, Edward Kennedy merits his reputation as godfather to America's immigration policy since 1965; his brother Robert served as witness before the subcommittee. But the Immigration Act of that year was more than an act of homage to the late president: It was substantially the legacy of the desegregation campaign in the 1950s, an extension of the civil rights movement of the 1960s, and of anticolonial sentiment following World War II. The legislation that produced the Civil Rights Law of 1964, and the amendments added to the McCarran-Walter Act the following year, wended their way through the same Congress and were approved by many of the same congressmen. By 1964 Rosa Parks, the Freedom Riders, and Martin Luther King Jr. were recognized gods in the pantheon created by a mythology more potent and influential even than immigration; it was the genius of the architects of immigration "reform" that they recognized the possibility for conflating the two and amalgamating them as statute law.

While a superficial contribution of the civil rights agenda to immigration reform was to stigmatize any expression or implied thought of racial preference, the fundamental one was the perception of an underlying symmetry between the condition of peoples of color in the former European colonies of Asia and Africa and native American blacks, including the obligations owed them by the United States. Religious groups especially were inclined to make this equation, as an editorial in the *Christian Century*—whose regular contributors included Reinhold Niebuhr, Seymour Martin Lipset, Martin E. Marty, and Martin Luther King Jr.—suggests. "We are in danger," the editors warned, "of preaching freedom and reveling in it ourselves but denying it to those who knock at our doors. . . . The denial borders on blasphemy at Bethlehem. Fling wide the gates and let some glory in." Interestingly, the connection between domestic racial relations and immigration was made as early as the middle of the nineteenth century by Senator Charles Sumner, the abolitionist, who wished to broaden the amendment of the naturalization statute by rewriting it in racially neutral terms so as to include the Chinese, as well as people of African race or descent. "[I]mmigrants' rights," a reader wrote to the *New York Times* several years ago, "are the civil rights of the 1990s. . . ." And indeed, many of the opponents of the Immigration Act of 1965 had opposed the Civil Rights Law of 1964, including Senator Sam Ervin, who anticipated a remark by

Patrick Buchanan nearly thirty years later when, in defending the national origins system, he admitted to not understanding why Ethiopia should be granted an annual quota equal to that of England or Germany.

Almost every supporter of the amendments to McCarran-Walter believed, or professed to believe, that they would effect very little change in immigration patterns and numbers, and that their importance was essentially symbolic. The idea, inchoate as it may have been, was that a national debt to internal parties should be paid off to external ones, only a small minority of whom were of the same color as the wronged domestic group. Human beings have a strange and contradictory inclination to regard past benefactions as imposing future obligations, not on the beneficiary but on the benefactor—and so it was, and is, with the United States in its relations with the rest of the world. The nation that had shifted the military balance against the aggressor powers in World War II; forced the European governments to disgorge their empires postwar; fought, with however mixed motives, for the cause of what it conceived at least to be freedom for remote peoples around the globe, and lavished foreign aid upon them—this country by the 1960s had come to be thought of as, morally speaking, the world's greatest debtor nation, most notably by itself! Whatever the sins of the white American majority against the black domestic minority, it is difficult to understand how they could have extended to black—or yellow, or red—majorities overseas; or how, if they did, settling the score with creditors abroad alleviated the plight of those at home. ("President Lyndon Johnson declared war on American poverty in 1964. Yet no irony was perceived the following year when LBJ and Congress agreed on sweeping new reform legislation that would step up the *importation* of poverty. Washington ignored the connections between immigration, economics, and poverty, preferring to extend the 1964 Civil Rights Act and the spirit of the 'Great Society' to the entire world.")[18] The answer seems to be that spectacular assumptions of moral guilt are very often acts of pride, itself the result of exaggerated self-importance and of hubris: qualities that, in the years of the New Frontier and the Great Society, became conspicuous in the United States of America.

The Johnson administration took to immigration reform like Baby Huey to water. In the opinion of the new president, the national origins system was "incompatible with our basic American tradition"—never mind the fact that, as Milton D. Morris notes, some form or another of it had existed for almost a century, and that it had served as the basis for the country's regulatory legislation since its inception.[19] Secretary of State Dean Rusk, testifying before the Senate Immigration Subcommittee in the summer of 1964, explained that, whereas Congress in 1924 had expected hordes of impoverished and untrained people would shortly overwhelm the United States, "Present day immigration is much different in volume and makeup. . . . Immigration now comes in limited volume and includes a relatively high proportion of older people, females and persons of high skill and training. . . . The action we urge . . . is not to make a drastic departure from a long-established immigration policy, but rather to reconcile our immigration policy as it has been developed in recent years with the letter of the general law"—meaning, of course, to bring the McCarran-Walter into line with the attorney general's parole authority. In a speech he delivered at St. Olaf College in Minnesota, Abba P. Schwartz, head of Security and Consular Affairs for the State Department, warned that "Our discriminatory immigration policies send the wrong message around the world," and accused organized labor and other opponents of reform of xenophobia. And Senator Hiram Fong of Hawaii stated in debate on the Senate floor one month before the act of 1965 passed that immigration, so far from being any longer "merely" a domestic issue, had great international significance as part of America's crusade against totalitarianism. "Until the racial incongruities of our present basic immigration laws which discriminate against certain national and ethnic groups are eliminated, our laws needlessly impede our struggle for global peace."

It has been charitably said that John F. Kennedy never envisioned chain migration (produced by family reunification) or the "push factor," and perhaps he did not, though prudence, or foresight, is supposed to be the chief virtue of the statesman. Johnson's attorney general, Nicholas DeB. Katzenbach, told the Senate subcommittee that the purpose of the amendments was not to increase immigration, but simply to do away with the discriminatory quotas: The Department of Labor expected the new legislation to add only 23,000 workers annually to the labor force. "First," intoned Senator Edward Kennedy, "our cities will not be flooded with a million immigrants annually. Under the proposed bill, the present level of immigration remains substantially the same. Secondly, the ethnic mix will not be upset. Contrary to charges in some quarters, it will not inundate America with immigrants from any one country or area." Senatorial disingenuousness was rife, in other words, up to and beyond the point of dishonesty, as it was elsewhere in government. Katzenbach and the Johnson administration, for instance, proposed a slight increase in the quota per annum from 158,000 to 166,000. The figure, however, represented only quota immigrants and did not include the nonquota ones—meaning immediate relatives of recently arrived immigrants and those who came from the Western Hemisphere before 1965. Moreover, the aforementioned quota was reserved strictly for immigrants from outside that hemisphere. Though the old quota had not been filled in some years, the Senators fully expected the new one to be filled entirely. Robert Kennedy estimated that the bill would result in "at most 50,000 [more immigrants] a year." Edward Kennedy suggested 62,000, and Senator Philip Hart of Michigan offered 66,000. Hart assured Katzenbach: "[T]he notion was created that 190 million [Americans] is [sic] going to be swallowed up. None of us would want that, the bill does not seek to do it and the bill could not do it."[20]

The publicity and general hype surrounding the unveiling of the Immigration and Nationality Act of 1965 contrasted with the simpler ceremony in which President Coolidge had affixed his signature to the Quota Law of 1924. President Johnson signed HR 2580 at the base of the Statue of Liberty on 3 October 1965, the while insisting that it was, after all, no big deal. "This bill that we sign today is not a revolutionary bill. It does not affect the lives of millions. It will not reshape the structure of our daily lives, or really add importantly to either our wealth or power." Rather, "This bill says simply that from this day forth those wishing to emigrate to America shall be admitted on the basis of their skills and their close relationship to those already here. . . . Our beautiful America was built by a nation of strangers. . . . And from this experience, almost unique in the history of nations, has come America's attitude toward the world. We, because of what we are, feel safer and stronger in a world as varied as the people who make it up—a world where no country rules another and all countries can deal with the basic problems of human dignity and deal with those problems in their own way. . . ."

The Immigration and Nationality Act of 1965, in retrospect, was among the American nation's grandest gestures and very likely its most costly one, immediately as in the long run. More significantly, it was gesture substituted for policy begetting a series of similar gestures, like the random signalings of an actor who has forgotten his part. The act of 1965 was based on no research, scientific or otherwise, nor did it follow, like the Quota Law of 1924, upon a long and intensive national debate. It embodied no formulated concept of the future demographic and economic needs of the United States, nor of its cultural and environmental health. At no time did the solons responsible for its passage consider what the material benefits to America of immigration might be, or how abuses might develop. The entire exercise brings to mind a saying of Lionel Trilling's, that the American academy is devoted to ideas, not to thinking, and that this matters because its ideas are adopted almost at once by the American political class. Formally speaking, the McCarran-Walter Act was the law of the land in respect of immigration from 1952 until 1990, when it was replaced by the Immigration Act of that year, signed by President George Bush. In practice, it was substantially ignored before its amendment in 1965 and almost entirely so between 1965 and 1990, as one "amendment" after another was tacked onto it until the original shape was finally obscured. These amendments include that of 1976 adjusting the National Origins Quota still further, the Refugee Act of 1980 establishing larger quotas for refugees, and the Immigration Control and Reform Act of 1986, which purported to address the problem of illegal immigration, though, as Lawrence Fuchs observes, it was essentially a pro-immigration bill, not a restrictive one. In the 1970s, two commissions—the so-called Rockefeller Commission, appointed by President Richard Nixon to study the feasibility and utility of a national population policy, and the Select Commission on Immigration and Refugee Policy, established by Congress and chaired by Fuchs—did consider a number of issues crucial to the design of a wise and prudent immigration policy, but the second resulted only in the 1980 Refugee Act, while the first achieved nothing at all. As for the act of 1990—which *increased* the quota for legal immigrants from 500,000 to 700,000 a year in 1992, 1993, and 1994—though it represented the first major reform of immigration law in a quarter of a century, it failed wholly to formulate a rationale for the large-scale immigration it made inevitable.

Unfortunately for the United States, its legislators are not interested in concrete questions and answers, such as, What should the goals of an intelligent American immigration policy be? They are interested in what Trilling pejoratively calls Ideas—that is, when they are not busy pursuing money, votes, and women. For them, immigrationism—which began as a component of a statist nationalism in the late nineteenth century, entwined itself with the humanitarian imperialism of the 1950s and '60s, and presently constitutes an indispensable element in the dream of multicultural globalism—is not an adopted policy but an ideological commitment whose origins trace from the years immediately following World War II, when the popular sentimentalities regarding a "nation of immigrants" hardened into ideological slogans propagated by bureaucrats looking to create what Clyde Wilson calls "a third form of American nationalism." Now that the United States has become the undisputed leader of the world, "For the first time the American leadership class, the politicians and intellectuals who were the inheritors of the Progressive Era's belief in elite and expert rule, in technique, optimism, and progress, began to regard American success not as an end but as a means."[21]

The American governing class is not only the creator of the immigrationist myth, it is its chief and (after Julian Simon and Ben Wattenberg) its most fervent propagator, as the one hundredth anniversary celebration of the Statue of Liberty—described by Max Lerner as "the American Empire at its showiest"—demonstrated. Early in the 1950s, the government proposed that a Museum of Immigration be erected on Bedloe's Island at the foot of the statue, and launched a fund drive for that purpose which spread the image of the Mother of Exiles nationwide. Significantly, the American public evinced no interest in the project, despite solicitations from celebrities who included Edward R. Murrow, Pierre S. Du Pont, Ed Sullivan, and the historian Allan Nevins. Eventually Congress in frustration coughed up the requisite monies, and the American Museum of Immigration opened in 1972, barely in time to welcome the immigrant hordes created by the Immigration Act of 1965. Owing to its appeal, or usefulness, to liberals and conservatives, Democrats and Republicans alike, the myth has become endemic within the federal government, and even the governments of certain states. "Can we doubt," Ronald Reagan asked rhetorically in accepting the Republican presidential nomination in 1980, "that only a Divine Providence placed this land, this island of freedom here as a refuge for all these people who yearn to breathe free? Jews and Christians enduring persecution behind the Iron Curtain; the boat people of Southeast Asia, Cuba, and of Haiti; the victims of drought and famine in Africa; the freedom fighters in Afghanistan." Alas, if Reagan believed that he was speaking for the conscience of America he was wrong; and if he thought his words represented the vision of the founders of the American Republic, he was wronger still.

NOTES

1. Henry Pratt Fairchild, *Immigration: A World Movement and Its American Significance* (New York: Macmillan, 1913), p. 51.
2. Lawrence H. Fuchs, "Immigration, Pluralism, and Public Policy: The Challenge of the Pluribus to the Unum," in Mary M. Kritz, ed., *U.S. Immigration and Refugee Policy: Global and Domestic Issues* (Lexington, Mass.: Lexington Books, 1983), pp. 294–95.
3. Cf. Clyde Wilson, "The Future of American Nationalism," *Chronicles: A Magazine of American Culture,* November 1990, pp. 16–21.
4. Thomas J. Curran, *Xenophobia and Immigration, 1820–1930* (Boston: Twayne Publishers, 1975), pp. 21, 150.
5. Wilson, "The Future of American Nationalism," pp. 17–18.
6. John Lukacs, *Immigration and Migration: A Historical Perspective* (Monterey, Va.: American Immigration Control Foundation, 1986), p. 10.
7. Christopher Lasch, *The True and Only Heaven: Progress and Its Critics* (New York: Norton, 1991), p. 206.
8. Morton White and Lucia White, *The Intellectual versus the City: From Jefferson to Frank Lloyd Wright* (New York: Oxford University Press, 1977), pp. 90–91, 95–97, 224–25.
9. Cf. Lasch, *The True and Only Heaven,* pp. 353–54.
10. Cf. White and White, *The Intellectual versus the City,* pp. 147–48, 162, 180, 183.
11. Cf. Wayne Lutton, *The Myth of Open Borders* (Monterey, Va.: American Immigration Control Foundation, 1988).

12. Julius Drachsler, *Democracy and Assimilation* (Westport, Conn.: Negro Universities Press, 1970; original publication, New York: Macmillan, 1920), p. 230.

13. John Lukacs, *Outgrowing Democracy: A History of the United States in the Twentieth Century* (New York: Doubleday, 1984), pp. 137–45.

14. Lasch, *The True and Only Heaven,* pp. 70–71.

15. John F. Kennedy, *A Nation of Immigrants* (New York and Evanston: Harper & Row, revised edition, 1964), p. 71.

16. Elizabeth A. Koed, "A Symbol Transformed: How 'Liberty Enlightening the World' Became 'The Mother of Exiles,'" *The Social Contract,* Spring 1992, pp. 134–39.

17. David W. Reimers, "Recent Immigration Policy: An Analysis," in Barry Chiswick, ed., *The Gateway: U.S. Immigration Issues and Policies* (Washington, D.C.: American Enterprise Institute for Public Policy Research, 1982), p. 18.

18. David Simcox, "Muddling Masses," *Chronicles: A Magazine of American Culture* January 1993, pp. 31–32.

19. Milton D. Morris, *Immigration: The Beleaguered Bureaucracy* (Washington, D.C.: The Brookings Institution, 1985), p. 40.

20. Lawrence Auster, *The Path to National Suicide* (Monterey, Va.: American Immigration Control Foundation, 1990), p. 13.

21. Wilson, "The Future of American Nationalism," pp. 19–20.

In addition to those sources cited above, works consulted in the preparation of this section include David Bennett, *The Party of Fear: From Nativist Movements to the New Right in American History* (Chapel Hill: University of North Carolina Press, 1988); Barbara Blumberg, *Celebrating the Immigrant: An Administrative History of the Statue of Liberty National Monument,* Cultural Resources Management Study No. 10 (Washington, D.C.: National Park Service, U.S. Department of the Interior, 1985); James Lincoln Collier, *The Rise of Selfishness in America* (New York: Oxford University Press, 1991); John R. Commons,

Races and Immigrants in America (New York: Macmillan, 1916); Robert A. Divine, *American Immigration Policy: 1924–1952* (New Haven, Conn.: Yale University Press, 1957); Roy Lawrence Garis, *Immigration Restriction* (New York: Macmillan, 1927); Otis L. Graham, *Illegal Immigration and the New Reform Movement* (Washington, D.C.: Federation for American Immigration Reform, 1980); John Higham, *Strangers in the Land: Patterns of American Nativism, 1860–1925* (New Brunswick, N.J.: Rutgers University Press, 1988); Richard D. Lamm and Gary Imhoff, *The Immigration Time Bomb: The Fragmenting of America* (New York: Dutton, 1985); Moses Rischin, ed., *Immigration and the American Tradition* (Indianapolis, Ind.: Bobbs-Merrill, 1976); Mary Shapiro, *Gateway to Liberty: The Story of the Statue of Liberty and Ellis Island* (New York: Vintage Books, 1987); and Rita J. Simon and Susan Alexander, *The Ambivalent Welcome: Print Media, Public Opinion and Immigration* (Westport, Conn.: Praeger, 1993).

See also "Trans-National America," Randolph Bourne, *The Radical Will: Selected Writings 1911–1918* (New York: Urizen Books, 1976), and Frederick Jackson Turner, "The Significance of the Frontier in American History," Occasional Paper Number 1 (Petoskey, Mich.: Social Contract Press, 1994).

III

MYSTIQUE OR MISTAKE?

"THE WORST, THE MOST CORRUPTING LIES," GEORGES Bernanos said, "are problems falsely stated." Confucius, asked what would be among his first acts if he were made head of state, replied, "Rectify the language." Problems falsely stated and a degraded language are significantly responsible for the silliness, triviality, and dishonesty of the contemporary debate on immigration, which M. E. Bradford compared to the worst plays of the last three centuries. In Australia—also a major country of immigration—the subject is discussed far more honestly and pragmatically than it is in the United States, and with much less squeamishness. The *Los Angeles Times* in 1992 worried that Governor Pete Wilson could be understood as blaming immigrants for California's financial difficulties. What Wilson should have been doing, the paper suggested, was to discuss the "troubling" demographic picture without mentioning immigrants at all. "The implication," says Lawrence Auster, "is that there exists some 'acceptable' way to speak critically about the immigration problem without 'exploiting' it. But since that advice comes from the very people who have never spoken about immigration except in glowing clichés, and who have always stigmatized anyone who did find fault with it, one wonders what this 'nonexploitive' way of discussing the issue might be." Again, Albert R. Hunt, an immigrationist commentator for the *Wall Street Journal,* has complained that while Wilson claims to be addressing the problem of illegal immigration, "his rhetoric tars all immigrants." Hunt's extralogical conclusion—that "it's one thing to try to stop illegal immigration at the border or the workplace; it's inconceivable to try to stop it in the schoolyard" by barring the children of illegals from a public education—is an obvious example of what Georgie Anne Geyer has in mind when she refers to the intellectual corruption that illegal immigration has produced in the United States among liberal, conservative, and religiously committed persons: among just about everyone, in fact. "The problem of illegals corrupts by destroying people's ability to think clearly." That the moral imperative to think clearly is as strong as the command to think charitably is a truth easily overlooked in a period dubbed by one critic as the age of conspicuous benevolence.

From 1981 to 1984, the Ninety-seventh and Ninety-eighth Congresses applied themselves to the subject of immigration in its historical context as they struggled with legislation introduced by Senators Simpson and Mazzoli. Those whose testimony was considered included numerous politicians and many spokesmen for an array of ethnic groups but only two historians, one of them a specialist in immigration. As the hearings proceeded, a consensus emerged on American history as an infolding of an immigrant rainbow, interrupted by eruptions of bigotry and intolerance embodied in restrictive legislation since proven to have been moral aberrations and historical mistakes, from which the country had learned its lesson. One by one, the opponents of a new set of reforms—Senator Edward Kennedy, Father Theodore Hesburgh, Donald Hohl of the U.S. Catholic Conference, the historian Loy Bilderback, who reminded his listeners that, historically, racism had been the primary motive force in American immigration policy—came forward to testify that "history teaches" that American values and ideals have entered the United States by way of the Golden Door, and to warn that the legislators must not "fly in the face of American history," as Senator Kennedy said. The congressmen were sandbagged by the general enthusiasm, which prevented them apparently from noticing that none of the historical testimony was historical at all, but purely anecdotal, sentimental, and analogic. In 1989 the Senate debate on legislation that became the Immigration Act of 1990 recapitulated this mishmash of what David Simcox described as "anecdotes, slogans, and impressions, vague notions about the nation's immigrant past, and a desire to use immigration law to affirm standards of charity and generosity." Utterly lost in the emotional haze was the smallest consideration for the national interest, including such pragmatic concerns as the likely effect of expanded immigration on population growth and natural resources. As Jean-François Revel has remarked, "Fear of knowing always leads to fear of calling things by their names."

Two sisters-in-law of a friend, both resident in the South, take it as an accepted fact that whites are a minority group in the United States, and that blacks in this country are the racial majority. Surrounded as they are by black faces, and subjected like everyone else in the nation to television's preoccupation with the doings and problems of black and brown Americans, theirs is a comprehensible delusion. Julian Simon attributes the unpopularity of immigration with the American people to what they read in the newspapers and see on TV, as well as to rabble-rousing by anti-immigrant organizations. He has made this astounding claim in the face of a clear and obvious bias in the American media toward immigrants and a generous immigration policy which, while it falls far short of suggesting that we are a nation of newly *arrived* immigrants, offers no ground for objecting to such a prospect. By their coverage and through their rhetoric, the print and electronic media display simultaneously sympathy for immigrants, susceptibility to the immigrationist myth, and disdain for the "mean-spiritedness" and "xenophobia" of their detractors. Garrett Hardin, who credits the news media with having played a major role in passing the 1990 Immigration Act (an "anti-democratic bill"), understands journalism's openness to immigration as an aspect of journalists' attraction to universalism or one-worldism, which he sees as "a natural, though fatal, inference from their craft": that of professional literates who assume that the sharing of information implies the sharing of wealth and territorial space. Besides the universalist temptation, the journalist's addiction to sentimentality, his tendency to personalize all stories and issues, and his infatuation with the new, the fashionable, and the futuristic help explain his immigrationist sensibilities. Whether purveyed through the newspapers and magazines or on television, the typical immigration-related story concerns a political victim with scars on his wrists being served with a deportation notice at the airport, or a large Mexican family being repatriated to Tijuana on a Border Patrol bus in the middle of the night. At any other level, the treatment of immigration is largely taboo in the American popular media.

American journalists' engagement with the immigration issue, being essentially a function of their self-image, reflects a moralistic approach to the subject rather than a conscientious one. Reporters for *Time* and *Newsweek*, both of which devoted entire issues to immigration and "cultural diversity" in 1993, work very, very hard to acknowledge undeniable particulars while swimming against the tide of American public opinion in respect of generalities, adopting a give-with-the-one-hand, take-with-the-other approach to the debate, which they combine with a tentative and usually faked conclusion. In the *Newsweek* for 9 August 1993, the authors of an article titled "The Economic Cost of Immigration," after asserting that two centuries of American history "seem to confirm" that "energetic workers increase the supply of goods and services with their labor, and increase the demand by spending their wages," admit that both the welfare state and the arrival of less-skilled immigrants since 1970 have "helped to undercut the benefits of immigration," and finish with a begged and inconclusive conclusion. "The welfare costs of immigration should dramatically decrease as the California and U.S. economies recover." (Why?) "The long-term benefits of immigrant labor and business enterprise will then be more apparent." (How so?) "But the age of innocence in the American immigration experience is over." (Whose innocence?) "The rise of the U.S. welfare state has placed a cushion under the immigrant experience—and diminished the benefits of immigration to the country at large." Another article in the same issue observes that Americans believe "with some justice" that the United States no longer controls its borders; also—erroneously, *Newsweek* says—that immigrants swell the welfare rolls and contribute disproportionately to crime in this country. "And they are clearly *uncomfortable* with the fact that almost all the New Immigration comes from Latin America, the Caribbean and Asia." (My emphasis.) Somehow it is hard to envy *Newsweek* writers their jobs.

By contrast, *Time*'s special issue in the fall of 1993 pulls all the stops in making its contribution to the controversy. "This issue of *Time,*" the editors explain in their introductory essay, "is devoted to American diversity, and thus by definition to the differences among Americans. Those differences gain their impact, however, from the bonds that unite them in one vast and variegated country. They are differences that should not divide or weaken America, but distinguish and strengthen it. They are the reason to keep the welcome mat, however worn or tattered at times, always ready at the door." *Time*'s unequivocal enthusiasm was made supportable by the editors' decision to avoid the social and economic effects of immigration and concentrate on multiculturalism and diversity, which, unlike the immigrants who contribute so substantially to them, are nowadays almost beyond criticism. "In ways that were hardly conceivable even a generation ago," Pico Iyer enthuses in his endpiece, "the new world order is a version of the New World writ large: a wide-open frontier of polyglot terms and postnational trends. A common multiculturalism links us all—call it Planet Hollywood, Planet Reebok or the United Colors of Benetton." Elsewhere in the issue mention appears that the Mandarin word for America is *Meiguo,* "the Beautiful Country," and Gloria Estefan is quoted as saying that "When immigrants come to America they bring their culture, and that culture becomes part of a new country. It makes everyone stronger." The editors pause briefly to acknowledge a Yankelovich poll they had commissioned, which found that three-quarters of the American public believes that immigration policy should be altered, and immigration itself restricted. They brighten, however. "Does this mean the end of the American pact with newcomers to its shores? Almost certainly not. Despite differences, recent immigrants have brought to the U.S. a diversity, a vitality, a freshness unseen since the vast immigration waves of the nineteenth century." As Dr. Johnson said, a man might write such stuff forever would he but *abandon his mind* to the task.

Over the past few years, a number of developments and events—among them California's fiscal crisis and the Los Angeles riots—have prompted many newspapers and television news programs at least to pretend to consider the extent to which immigration may have been a contributing factor to these debacles. In 1992 the *Atlantic Monthly* printed a long essay by Jack Miles, spoiled Jesuit and former editor of the *Los Angeles Times*'s Sunday book review, which the *Washington Post* commended for the author's ability to maintain ideological purity while breaking from ideological stricture. "It is a marshaling of analysis and statistic, as well as his personal experience . . . that in the end leads him to call for a profound revolution of immigration policy. . . . This leads Miles to conclude, against powerful contrary instincts, that controlling the influx of immigrants may be the only way to rescue the underclass, particularly the black underclass, in the United States today."

But the American media's preferred means of handling the immigration question is what Roy Beck, Washington correspondent for the *Social Contract,* calls "Afghanistanism"—the examination of a problem thematically close to home as it manifests itself in a distant country. The device is scarcely a new one, having been developed centuries ago as a prudential way of criticizing domestic political conditions by re-creating them in foreign or even mythical lands. What *is* new is that this particular exercise in *eloignement* is entirely self-imposed. Thus a cover story in the *New York Times Magazine* mused, "Are European societies destined to . . . become multi-racial and multi-ethnic? Are Europeans willing to accept such a transformation? Do they have the means and the power to prevent it, even if they want to?" The following year, a *Times* editorial concluded that tightening asylum regulations in Germany was a "reasonable" step for the government to take; though, as Ira Mehlman pointed out, evidence of fraud on the grand scale and simple terrorism was required before the paper felt comfortable in reaching the same conclusion regarding American asylum policy. Similarly, when the Miles article and one by Peter Brimelow in *National Review* advocating a reformulation of immigration law appeared, such mainstream publications as

U.S. News and World Report gave them notice, in this way bringing to the attention of their readers arguments that they would not have dared broach on their own, and for which they were not prepared to accept responsibility. "Whatever apprehensions the U.S. media had about the direction of American immigration policy were best expressed by assigning them to outside observers. They could accomplish this by reporting about how others viewed the United States. . . . In other words, it was not the *Times* that thought America was plagued by ethnic and racial tensions, people in Europe did. The *Times* was merely reporting what foreigners thought about the state of our society."[1]

The power of the immigrationist myth, and a desire to avoid political incorrectness, have so far maintained the widespread reluctance on the part of genuine intellectuals, as well as of the intellectually *nouveaux riches,* to sophisticate the immigration debate by lifting it above the elementary moral level of personal fairness and victimology. This is true especially of liberal immigrationists, who must surely have grasped by now the extent to which the liberal agendum is far more Eurocentric than many or most of its adherents care to admit. (For instance, the animal rights movement is not the creation of Mexican immigrants, many of whom are *aficionados* of the *corrida* at home, but of the descendants of those elderly British ladies in doormat tweeds, who would happily have sacrificed the better part of the human race for their dogs.) Robert Royal, in *1492 and All That: Political Manipulations of History,* reminds his readers that pluralism itself is a distinctively European idea. "The wish to contest an allegedly monolithic European view of history with fresh voices and perspectives inescapably belongs to a very European mode of thought," as the European imaginative and intellectual response to the early explorations of the New World attests. It is not the traditional values of dead white European males only, but those of the American Left itself, that are threatened by the opposing values that non-European and Third World immigrants bring with them—something that leftists intuitively comprehend, but that they dare not protest or even, perhaps, admit to themselves. For liberals as well as conservatives, for Jews as well as WASPs, for Mexican-Americans as well as for blacks, the immigration dilemma poses more than so many individual moral claims against a collective and selfish one; rather it sets an array of broader claims against a roster of equally broad ones. The result, depending on how one views it, is rampant hypocrisy, or the intellectual corruption that Georgie Anne Geyer protests.

Robert Reinhold of the *New York Times,* in an article composed of a series of sentimental vignettes of illegal aliens looking forward to being amnestied and reflecting on their underground life in "their chosen land," wrote with special sympathy of Marcelino Castro of Zecatepec, Mexico. "Now he wants to start his own business and become an American citizen. He already owns two color television sets and a cordless telephone and is a fervent Dallas Cowboys fan." Nice for Señor Castro; but how strange to find the high-mindedly antimaterialist, anticonsumerist, and frequently anticapitalist *Times* boasting that America has taken a noble Mexican *paisano* and changed him into a materialist, a consumerist, and a sports fan—an American redneck, in short! Even Anna Quindlen allowed righteous anger at the passage of Proposition 187 in California to betray her into writing a wholly unwonted dithyramb to the United States of America. "Sure, they [the illegal immigrants] came here to strike it rich. But many of them believed that America was in some deeper sense a better place, a place that had elevated the dignity of man to a governmental art form." If these people were wrong, Quindlen didn't bother to correct them.

On every kind of issue, the immigrationists' defense of immigration directly contradicts other of their enthusiasms. *Secularization:* As even *Time* admits, large numbers of immigrants of whatever religious persuasion oppose the displacement of the Deity from public life by the subterfuge of "separation of church and state" as strongly as do native Christian fundamentalists, and can be expected in time to protest it as aggressively if American culture does not succeed in paganizing them first. *Feminism:* Immigrants in increasing numbers arrive from cultures that regard women as the possessions of their husbands, with no business to be in school or working outside the home. When a Chinese immigrant in New York City killed his wife with a hammer for her infidelity, feminists were outraged; when a Somali woman in Georgia performed a clitorectomy on her two-year-old niece, they were if possible more outraged still. Commenting on the behavior of alien cabbies in Chicago, a spokeswoman for the city explained, "They treat women worse than anyone. Maybe it's part of their cultures that women are beneath them. Whatever the reason, they're either trying to seduce them or bully them." *Environmentalism:* Senator Gary Hart, ordinarily sympathetic to environmental concerns, ignored the connection between immigration and population growth in his bid for the Democratic presidential nomination in 1984, and, citing the supposed dangers it posed to civil rights, voted against the Simpson-Mazzoli bill. *Animal rights:* In Florida and in Los Angeles, disputes have led to legal confrontations between local authorities attempting to outlaw animal sacrifice and Santeria, an Afro-Cuban cult which performs such sacrifices as part of its regular worship services and insists that civil ordinances against the practice violate its First Amendment rights.

Newsweek's Tom Morgenthau several years ago described Senator Dianne Feinstein as "scrambling to neutralize nativist backlash." Of course, her "scrambling" was for tactical purposes only! Feinstein—a woman, a feminist, a Jew, a Democrat, a liberal—couldn't be an anti-immigrationist—a *nativist!* No wonder nobody at *Newsweek,* as almost everywhere else, has an interest in stating the problem of immigration correctly.

THE IMMIGRATIONIST MYTH IS RADICALLY CONNECTED WITH the myth of American exceptionalism, which is almost the precondition for its emergence. Carl Schurz, a German immigrant who arrived in the United States after the failed revolutions in 1848, commanded a division at Second Bull Run, and served as secretary of the interior under President Rutherford B. Hayes, assured an assembly of political leaders in Boston that "a new country has opened its boundless fields to those great ideas, for the realization of which the old world seems no longer to be wide enough. It is as though the earth herself had taken part in the general revolution, and had thrown up from her sea-covered womb a new battle-ground for the spirit of the new era. That is America. Not only the invention of gunpowder and of the printing press, but also the discovery of America, inaugurates the modern age." Abraham Lincoln saw Americans as "an almost chosen people" and the English poet John Masefield called them "a wondrous race," while R. W. B. Lewis described the popular image of the American of more than a century ago as "a figure of heroic innocence and vast potentialities, poised at the start of a new history." In recent times, Jerry Falwell has claimed that God blessed the United States for its devotion to Him and the Bible at the beginning of its history, that the founders believed that America had a special destiny to fulfill in the world, and that today the nation, having "more God-fearing citizens per capita than any other nation on earth," is the "last logical base for World evangelization." Kirkpatrick Sale, the Deep Ecologist and revisionist chronicler of the era of discovery, implicitly accepts the exceptionalist myth, embracing it as Br'er Rabbit embraced the tar baby when he accuses the

European explorers and settlers of forfeiting the chance for the peoples of Europe to create a new society in a new country, and through it to redeem the world.

The notion of American exceptionalism has been held in the past by liberals and conservatives, immigrationists and restrictionists, and continues to enjoy the favor of incompatible enthusiasts today. America has always seemed to some too exceptional to share, while others have thought it too special to keep for themselves; one historian, Robert A. Divine, has ascribed the isolationist movement of the 1920s and '30s to fear of contamination by the godless world beyond America's borders. Such fears are generally treated as attributes of the political Right in the United States. Yet Henry Luce—never a figure whom the Left has sought to claim for its own—established himself as the Mother Teresa of the global ideological slums when his article "The American Century" appeared in *Life* in 1941. "Ours," Luce declared, "must be the vision of many. It must be a sharing with all peoples our Bill of Rights, our Declaration of Independence, our Constitution.... It must be an internationalism of the people, by the people, and for the people.... For the moment, it may be enough to be the sanctuary of these ideals. But not for long." In the past decade and a half, "exporting the American Revolution" has been a catchphrase not of the Left but of the Right, owing to the enormous influence that neoconservative intellectuals gained within the Reagan administration. For Gregory Fossedahl, the "democratic idea," like Faith, is a divine gift which we do not merit personally and which we are morally obliged to communicate to, and share with, others. "[T]he extension of the democratic idea is ... the essence and raison d'etre of America itself." (Fossedahl, an ardent immigrationist, is scornful of what he calls "unfocused public xenophobia.")[2] In recent years, however, the validity of American exceptionalism as an historical concept has been reexamined, by liberals as well as by conservatives. Daniel Boorstin, the historical profession's Norman Vincent Peale, sticks to his guns, but Henry Kissinger in his *Memoirs* notes that while Theodore Roosevelt had accepted the premise that the United States was a nation among nations, obliged like them to pursue its own best interest, Woodrow Wilson conceived the "unprecedented doctrine" that American security was identical with the security of the entire world. The revisionist diplomatic historian William Appleman Williams predicted that Americans are at last destined to share the fate of mankind, while John Lukacs laconically insists that the history of the United States has *always* been inseparable from the history of Western civilization. As was true of Williams, Lukacs does not work particularly hard to disguise his half-amused contempt for so smug, self-satisfied, and historically naive an idea as American exceptionalism.

The novels of William Faulkner portray a region whose very ground is cursed by slavery. While the peculiar institution was restricted to the South and certain aggrandizing territories, racial antagonism of course was not; and it may well be that race is the virus that will prove fatal to even the pretense of exceptionalism in America. "In the very indeterminateness," George Kennan suggests, "—in the limitations of our vision and our power—there lies the same tragic quality that has always marked the great moments of human history. And in this sense America, if a great country, is also a tragic one." Exporting American democracy. . . . By importing the world? This is tantamount to a demand for universalism on the ground of American exceptionalism, which is really a contradiction in terms. Do American universalists mean to imply that *only* Americans should think universally? What propounders of the doctrine mean is that the genius of American government and American society is unique in the world. But what the American founders and the early Republicans understood by exceptionalism was that America's geographic position and condition—its separation by ocean from Europe; the availability of seemingly limitless amounts of land—permitted a new nation designed from classical republican principle and British constitutional law to hope for unprecedented potentialities, so long as the original geographic and demographic conditions obtained. America has *always* been unique; but it has *never* been exceptional. Denial of American exceptionalism is widely perceived as an act of cynicism or of selfishness, hinting at moral obtuseness. In fact, the reverse is more likely to be true.

The current debate on immigration is a dramatic example of public intellect subordinated to an aggravated conscience, which in this case happens to be a false conscience as well. The doctrinal aspect of American nationalism has historically been self-conscious; perhaps, as has been suggested, in part because the founding generation felt a need to justify and rationalize the break with the home country.[3] Similarly, American society is and always has been self-conscious; and the American conscience a self-conscious conscience. It is true that the "American conscience" is really many grouped consciences, some with overlapping, others with contradictory, concerns; also that one must distinguish between a public conscience and a popular one. But while the debate proceeds at a single level of American society, sentiment regarding immigration exists at all levels, and so does the moral self-inflation that hides behind self-consciousness. "For five hundred years, America has been the biggest story in the world." The words are Ben Wattenberg's, but the sentiment is probably shared by a majority of the American public, including that part of it that is restrictionist. "When it comes to immigration policy," says Alan Dowty, "the United States, like Caesar's wife, should be above suspicion." That statement seems to suggest, but in fact does not, moral humility, nor does it indicate depths of historical understanding on the part of the writer, who is the author of a recently published book attacking what he perceives as the assault on the right of freedom of movement around the world. Its ahistoricism, however, represents a significant flaw in American thought—one shared, on occasion, even by that consummate realist John Adams, who in an unguarded moment spoke of the United States as "a beacon on the summit of the mountains to which all the inhabitants of the earth may turn their eyes for a genial and saving light till time shall be lost in eternity, and this globe itself dissolves, nor leave a wreck behind." The United States in 1996 is far from being the vigorous, self-confident, and optimistic society that it was in 1896 yet, now as then, the overwhelming majority of Americans believes that American citizenship is the greatest good that can befall a human being in this world.[4] This amazing conceit is the result of a lingering assurance of the old republican virtue, compounded, in the past century, by the confusion of riches, power, and good fortune with innate virtue.

If today the immigration debate seems to be mostly an exercise in moralistic posturing and gesticulation, performed as much for the speaker's self-gratification as for the enlightenment of his listeners, that is because the immigrationist myth, abetted by conspicuous benevolence, has made the display of moral worth, both to ourselves and to the world, our immigration policy.[5] Wattenberg, who suffers from the inexplicable delusion that America and Americans are universally loved, for themselves as well as for their Hollywood culture, doubts not but that the world accepts us at our self-assigned value. He is among those people who Julian Simon insists would feel scorned and hurt should immigrants no longer wish to come to the United States. Unwelcome as it is in the present climate to suggest that our "responsibility" for solving the problems of other nations and foreign peoples is self-identified and self-imposed, in truth the assumption of such a duty is worse than misguided, it is hubristic. Concerned that the word "super-power" may have been superannuated by the collapse of bipolar international politics, Wattenberg opened his newspaper column to a contest whose purpose was to discover the most appropriate term with which to replace it. From among his favorite entries, including "hyper-power," "magna-power," "maxi-power," "mega-power," "multi-power," "semper power," "solo power," "supra-power," "ultra-power," and "uni-power," he chose . . . "omni-power"—as in "universal," he explained—thus raising the question of whether Ben Wattenberg is a benign imperialist, or only an idolator. Soon perhaps he will suggest changing the printing on our currency from "In God We Trust" to "God We Are." The federal government, which has already replaced God in the role of supplier of all good things to its 260 million subjects, now attempts to extend its beneficence to the nearly 4.75 billion people presently residing outside its territorial limits, as the theology of the state continues to replace the theology of the churches. "America is eternal," President Reagan asserted, to deafening silence from the Religious Right. One nation, indivisible, under God. . . . The words express a commitment to historical and metaphysical realities that by itself constitutes the supreme act of the American conscience, which is presently permitting itself to be diverted into fantastical byways and historical *cul-de-sacs*.

During the past century the United States, whose government was established as an act of defiance of governmental tyranny, has increasingly confused the quest for political freedom with the search for existential liberation, and sought to convert the American dream into a catchall for every fantasy and (frequently illicit) desire in human history. The predictable result is the encroachment of political fantasy on state policy, as with Julian Simon's repeated assertion that immigration is a "foolproof" means of advancing every major national goal and ensuring America's continued economic success. But John Lukacs, himself an immigrant from occupied Hungary in 1946, sees the United States not as a quintessentially new country, "the biggest story in the world," but rather as a very old one, shackled by realities of loss and of human tragedy that it prefers to deny. In this regard, at least, the immigrants really *are* superior to native Americans, arriving with a sense of fundamental reality that, among other things, makes them quite capable of imagining that we might wish rather to reject than to accept them. In the spring of 1995 Representative Dick Armey introduced an amendment to a House bill making scores of millions of Chinese eligible for refugee status in the United States on the ground that they faced forced abortion and sterilization at home. There is no better example of the unwillingness of the American ruling class, blinded by what Reinhold Niebuhr in the 1950s deplored as "moral perfectionism," to recognize limits to anything. Ellis Island is said to have been founded on an ideal. That is supposed to clinch the question of immigration. As Irving Babbitt remarked in the 1920s, "The outstanding trait of the men of our period may seem in retrospect to have been the facility with which they put forth untried conceits as 'ideals.'"

Dianne Feinstein thinks that legal immigration to America must be maintained as an achievable dream for people around the world, while *Time* compares American immigration to a book without an ending. And indeed, hardly anyone—even the most hard-nosed critic—suggests that it is time that the United States halted immigration for good. Instead, the advocate of immigration reform typically restricts himself to the suggestion that "America needs to consider a moratorium on immigration, until. . . ." The unreality of the immigrationist argument is manifest in its conclusion that, for the benefits of immigration to be sustained beyond a relatively brief period in the future, *immigration must continue at its present high levels forever.* Richard Rodriguez explains: "The trouble is, we never measure up. We, the children of immigrants, are never as bold, never as driven as our grandparents. That is why we become amazed sometimes by immigrant ambition." That is to say, as immigrants are Americanized—"assimilated"—they become corrupted by American laziness and American softness, and have to be replaced in the next generation by new waves of hardworking foreigners. The diversity argument holds the same implications—even partial assimilation produces a boring uniformity, requiring continuous infusions of ever more exotic peoples from unheard-of places—and so does the population argument. (Some have suggested that since, by one means of reckoning, the ratio between foreign- and native-born inhabitants is lower today than it was in 1910, the United States ought to accept a steadily growing number of immigrants to maintain an historically ordained ratio, as the total population of the country increases.) So, finally, does the case for accepting more refugees. Complaining that the message of American refugee policy is "When you can't get out, you can come in—but when you can get out, you can't get in," Wattenberg has urged that case-by-case approval by the State Department should revert to the blanket approval it replaced after the liberalization of the former Soviet bloc—an event, one might think, which would obviate claims to refugee status from that source. After the Polish government began seriously to persecute Solidarity in 1981, the U. S. government under its Extended Voluntary Departure

Program allowed thousands of Poles to remain in the United States "until conditions improved in that country." By 1990 Solidarity *was* the government in Poland, yet Washington made no move to repatriate the refugees, who preferred the good life in America to the travail of establishing freedom at home.[6] The slogan of the dedicated immigrationist is always, "Immigration Now, Immigration Forever!" For him, there is neither reason nor excuse for less immigration, in any humanly conceivable circumstance.

"KINDNESS AND TRUTH SHALL MEET," SAYS THE PSALMIST. The American public class at the end of the twentieth century is mostly opposed to truth, little concerned with kindness (which is not the same thing as "compassion"), but obsessed by "fairness," a legacy received in part from the economic redistributionism of the New Deal and, much more importantly, from the civil rights movement of the 1950s and '60s. Ironically, the president who once remarked *à propos* the Selective Service System that "Life is unfair" is the same who insisted upon bringing fairness to bear on the immigration policy of the United States. Since World War II, Washington has pursued a naive and futile quest for absolute fairness in respect of immigration without seriously considering the question "Fair to whom?" as if the answer were plain to see. In fact, no criterion for admission to the United States has escaped charges of discrimination, including selection for skills. The immigrationist myth and the ideology of rights, in combination and driven by the spirit of moral perfectionism, have succeeded in paralyzing efforts—including those of the U.S. Commission on Immigration Reform, chaired by the late Barbara Jordan—to revise the present system, and in intimidating those people who would prefer an otherwise candid discussion of revision.

Immigration is a crisis not for the United States alone, but for Canada, Australia, New Zealand, the Caribbean, and the nations of western Europe as well. While some of these countries are doing better than the United States, none is meeting the problem effectively, or with any kind of assurance. After studying the creation and implementation of immigration policy by their governments for twenty years, David North, director of the Center for Labor and Migration Studies at the New TransCentury Foundation in Washington, D.C., has concluded that the democracies are simply unwilling to spend sufficient monies or be tough-minded enough to control international migration. In North's opinion, guilt causes governments to shift the focus of debate from the harm that illegal immigration does the receiving countries to the international acceptability of the means to prevent it. Still, the treatment that immigration receives in the United States is distinguished by a scrupulosity with regard to "rights" and "fairness" that is matched nowhere else in the world. California's Proposition 187, for instance, was widely denounced for its provision that the public schools be required to verify the eligibility of the students, though proof of legal residency does not differ in principle from proof of residency within the school district. "I've lived as a legal resident alien in two countries, Switzerland and China. Now China really is a police state. But believe me, the fact that as a visually identifiable minority I was constantly being required to prove my resident status came a long way down on my list of things to worry about."[7] These reflections by a woman newspaper columnist based in California failed apparently to occur to Judge Steven Reinhardt of the Ninth U.S. Circuit Court of Appeals when he overturned an order to deport an illegal alien from Nigeria, writing in his opinion that the Immigration and Naturalization Service had unfairly investigated the gentleman on account of his "foreign-sounding" name. Justice William Brennan, in his decision in *Plyler v. Doe* (1982)—which declared unconstitutional the state of Texas's refusal to educate the children of illegal parents in the public school system— argued that lax enforcement of the immigration laws and the failure to devise an effective means of preventing the employment of illegals, added to the federal government's reluctance to deport them, amounted to "an inchoate federal permission to remain." A *New York Times* writer entangled himself in the Laocoön clutch of the fairness dilemma when he mused, "Fairness ought to be the main consideration. But often, fairness collides with the desire to respond to a highly visible plight—as demonstrated by recent decisions that seem to favor the admission of [Jewish and Armenian] refugees from the Soviet Union while restricting entry for those from Central America.... Still, why bend the rules for some foreigners and not others?"[8]

The Supreme Court noted in 1976 that Congress has regularly made law in respect of immigrants that it would find unacceptable if applied to American citizens. Professor Louis Henkin, writing in the *Harvard Law Review,* calls it inconceivable that the Court today should acquiesce in congressional acts comparable to Chinese Exclusion, which he describes as "a relic from a different era," when "orotund generalities about sovereignty and national security were a substitute for significant scrutiny of governmental action impinging on our individual rights; when the Bill of Rights had not yet become our national hallmark and the principal justification and preoccupation of judicial review...." Peter H. Schuck agrees that immigration has for many years been "a maverick, a wild card, in our public law," to the extent that "[p]robably no other area of American law has been so radically insulated and divergent from those fundamental norms of constitutional right, administrative procedure, and judicial role that animate our legal system."[9] All this ignores the fact that the statesmen of the early American Republic, including the framers, were careful to banish speculation regarding abstract rights from their discussion of immigration. Gouverneur Morris, for instance, believed that great nations, equally with social clubs, had the right to determine qualifications for membership.

A crucial difference between our own time and the founding era is the replacement of communitarianism by individualism, even by atomism. "The American mind is remarkably addicted to particularism, to making discrete judgments on matters considered individually."[10] An exaggerated individualism based on "rights-talk" permeates American government as well as the society it directs, creating an obsession with the individual (though often not the collective) rights of its citizens that has come to include the rights and privileges of noncitizens, here and abroad. This obsession makes it difficult for the governing and explaining classes to recognize the holistic nature of the immigration problem: the necessarily limited scope of the argument from "rights" itself, which in respect of immigration needs to be subordinated to other arguments having to do with constitutional, political, social, environmental, and economic considerations, and therefore of American liberality and generosity.[11] Robert F. Kennedy thought that the chief problem with American immigration law as it stood before 1965 was its failure to recognize that individuals have rights apart from their citizenship, and that the "community" in question in the immigration debate was not the nation only but men of goodwill everywhere. Today the problem is that influential people within the government and outside it refuse to distinguish between the rights of guests, intruders, and citizens, and to make the political decisions that such distinctions would require.

Immigrationists believe that "intersubjective values" rooted in the liberal tradition that they claim is synonymous with the American tradition form the basis for argument on behalf of a just immigration policy. According to their view, these values represent a kind of general will that forms a substantial part of the national interest, against which the restrictionists, whether intentionally or not, are contending. But the values to which they refer represent only a limited portion of the American consensus, or interest; and while a generous immigration policy may satisfy such American "ideals" as freedom, equality, and fairness, it is detrimental to others, including religious agreement, the preservation of cultural and intellectual tradition, and an intact ethnic core. Some defenders of immigration insist that a "nation of immigrants" like the United States has—unlike Japan or Ireland—no real racial, ethnic, or cultural identity, and therefore no true community to protect. However, certain liberals have recognized the validity of a defense of communitarianism developed from liberal principles. Frederick G. Whelan, for example, has suggested that Mill's axiom—that cultural vitality and progress result from any number of independent individuals separately pursuing their own ends—can be used to defend the diversity of nations, and that while one strain of liberalism does proceed logically to the concept of open borders, another recognizes the importance of fixed ones in maintaining and improving existing liberal societies.[12]

In today's America, the question of "rights" is never far removed from a concern for "civil rights"; since immigration law is fundamentally a matter of "discrimination," the connection has been significantly responsible for tenderizing and confusing the American conscience in respect of immigration itself. As early as the 1840s critics denied that the Constitution permitted the U.S. government to pass naturalization laws favoring immigrants from one nation over those from another, or immigrants of certain classes from within a single nation. But as immigration swelled to crisis proportions following the Civil War, and the quality of the immigrants changed with their countries of origin, both the legislative and judicial branches sought to establish a differing point of view in law. In its decision upholding the Chinese Exclusion Act of 1892, the Supreme Court recognized an inherent sovereign authority on the part of the federal government to exclude "foreigners of a different race in this country who will not assimilate with us," and were therefore potentially "dangerous to [the] peace and security of the country." Thirty years after the Quota Laws, elite opinion shifted toward an increasingly fashionable racial consciousness that replaced a generalized bias against people of color with an equally generalized bias in favor of them. "The idea," President Truman said in his message vetoing the Immigration and Nationality Act, "behind this discriminatory policy was, to put it boldly, that Americans with English or Irish names were better people and better citizens than Americans with Italian or Greek or Polish names. . . . Such a concept is utterly unworthy of our traditions and our ideals." This is an early expression of what Auster calls the "theoretical choice" between "equality and racism," the "actual choice" being between maintaining the existing ethnic composition of the nation and altering it fundamentally. "When the 1965 immigration reformers spoke of equal treatment before the law they meant it in terms of *individuals,* not in terms of mass migrations that would totally change the country. But today, with the rise of multiculturalism, we have lost the ability to make that basic distinction. The idea of equality has been transformed, in effect, from individuals to entire *cultures*. . . . Under this new dispensation we owe, as it were, an obligation to all the peoples in the world to let them migrate here en masse and recreate American society in their image." So great, it seems, is the scrupulosity of the antidiscriminators that the only way for the United States to avoid even the appearance of discrimination is to accept no immigrants at all, from anywhere.

If establishing race as the basis for admission is racism, why is not the substitution of family connections for race nepotism? Commentators as ideologically disparate as Governor Lamm and the *New Republic* have raised the question. President Johnson in his State of the Union Address in 1964 said that the United States ought to consider less an immigrant's native country and more what he could be expected to contribute to his adoptive one, a statement that his attorney general echoed. In 1965, the Immigration and Naturalization Service had identified five or six thousand cases of family separation. These, Senator Ervin argued, could be dealt with in ways that did not include rewriting American immigration law: "[W]e could cure any such injustice without changing the status of all the countries on earth." The act then taking shape in Congress, he claimed, did not do away with discrimination but merely transferred it from nontraditional immigrant groups to traditional ones. Though Ervin was ignored by his Senate colleagues, his objection was entirely valid. Johnson, Katzenbach, et al. to the contrary, the Immigration Act of 1965 was not primarily concerned with an immigrant's potential to make a contribution to the United States, but rather with whom he was separated from, which is simply national origin differently considered. The law as it stood before 1965 allotted 50 percent of the annual immigrant quota to skilled workers, 30 percent to the parents and unmarried adult children of naturalized American citizens, and 20 percent to spouses or unmarried children of permanent legal residents. As Auster notes, the new law reversed that priority by favoring relatives over skilled nonrelations. Today critics from the immigrationist as well as the restrictionist camp—for instance, Ben Wattenberg and Thomas Fleming—advocate replacing family unification with the importation of skills as the chief priority ("not," Fleming adds, "because [skilled immigrants] will make money for IBM, but because bright and able people are a precious and scarce commodity"). As early as 1965, however, egalitarians were charging that immigration "reform" threatened to replace racial prejudice with prejudice against the unskilled. They continue to do so to this day. "[I]t has become nearly impossible," the editors of the *New Republic* complain, "for those without connections to enter the country legally. There is no room for people who simply want to do what our ancestors did, come to America and try their luck. No wonder so many 'opportunity immigrants'—from Mexico, Yugoslavia, India, China, and elsewhere—choose to break the law."

Likewise no moral consensus has emerged on refugee and asylum policy but rather exaggerated disagreement, since refugees and applicants for asylum are in effect emergency immigrants whose cases require immediate evaluation and action, while entailing all the considerations presented by ordinary applicants. In deciding whether to accept or reject the pleas of refugees, the government is consistently subject to complaints that its motives are selfish ones, and also to charges that they are insufficiently so. Otis Graham, mocking the Carter administration's belief that it was "winning some sort of international victory" by accepting the Mariel boat people, wants the State Department to pay greater attention to the benefits that refugees might bring to the United States, less to the psychic satisfactions obtained by "affirmations of American-ness, expressions of national generosity, and votes of confidence in growth and change." On the other hand, the American tendency to view differences between competing states as fundamentally ideological disagreements has solidified into a conviction that people leave their home countries primarily for ideological reasons, and that we should therefore accept them as comrades-in-arms. In between are those who regard America's asylum policy as discriminatory, since it bases its selection process not on the suffering of the applicants but rather on the geopolitical benefits available to the United States. In an attempt to answer this last criticism Congress passed the Refugee Act of 1980, which altered the definition of "refugee" from that of a person fleeing persecution by a Communist or Communist-dominated country to that of one fleeing *any* country as a result of "persecution or a well-grounded fear of persecution on account of race, religion, nationality, membership in a particular social group, or political opinion." Certain writers have chosen to accept this idealistic and essentially symbolic piece of legislation as a formal acknowledgment that the United States recognizes the existence of universal rights to which American law must conform. In their opinion, America is morally obligated to accept as many refugees as wish to come here without jeopardizing vital interests, including the availability of jobs and housing, the national standard of living, and environmental health. The American government should ask its citizens to accept personal sacrifice to meet the impersonal demands that the national commitment to refugees imposes on them.[13]

In the context of immigration, the argument from rights and fairness emphasizes a personal concern for individual immigrants, while overlooking the communitarian interests of the native population. "In a universe that takes morals seriously, only certain reasons count."[14] Granted. But reasons drawn from considerations of personal happiness and individual fairness are not the only moral ones. The moral dilemma created by the immigration crisis is painful because it sets the valid moral claims of individuals against those of nations and peoples. (Though, as Aristotle wrote, the good of the whole advances the good of the individual, which is dependent upon it.) And increasingly, these individuals present themselves for admission not as individuals or even groups of individuals but as a mass, or masses. As Garrett Hardin says, "Numbers count." To be anti-immigration is not the equivalent of being anti-immigrant. Three generations ago, Henry Pratt Fairchild acknowledged the appeal of *laissez-faire* doctrine applied to immigration. "This probably accounts in large measure for its great vogue. The broad-minded and liberal man says, 'What can be better or more just than to let each individual work out his own destiny in the way that seems to him best?' Particularly does such a tremendous movement as modern immigration inspire the student with feelings of reverential awe, rather than a desire to intermeddle." But *laissez-faire* was insufficient to the problems of modern industrial life, and so, Fairchild concluded, is it unequal to the problems created in an age of mass migration. Libertarians, being strong believers in *laissez-faire* doctrine, tend to the immigrationist position. Many of them, including Julian Simon, impute an illegitimacy to the will and interests of corporate society, while accepting those of oppressed or alienated individuals as worthy of solicitude. At the close of the twentieth century, notions of community as understood by the elite classes are shifting worldwide to embrace the global society, open borders, freedom of trade and of movement, universal rights, and interchangeable citizenship. Yet, the further these ideas spread, the more tenuous their relation to reality is shown to be; in the former Yugoslavia, the former Soviet Union, in Africa, and also in the United States. As Peter Schuck says, "even a liberal nation has powerful propensities to exclude." The United States today sorely requires a moral consensus on immigration; and just as the communitarian argument alone can provide it, so only can exclusion for the purpose of what Michael Walzer calls "communities of character" sustain that consensus as well as, in the long run, the American nation itself. But a civilization that believes destruction to be the just reward of a society that fails to achieve moral perfection is certain, sooner or later, to gain that reward.

THE MODERN WORLD, NIETZSCHE SAID, IS OBSESSED WITH becoming, while ignoring being. Nathan Glazer calls the United States "the permanently unfinished country"; Julius Drachsler dedicated *Democracy and Assimilation* "To All Who Love America Not Alone For What She Is But For What She Could Be." Recently a Chinese-Hawaiian girl, a freshman at Occidental College in Los Angeles, told a reporter from the *Wall Street Journal* who had asked her how she would grade America that she would give it an incomplete. Immigrationism in the 1980s and '90s, like boosterism in the 1920s, is a type of Babbittry, though immigrationists—unlike Rotary and the Chamber of Commerce—are motivated less by optimism than by despair, at times even by hatred; something that their rhetoric is designed to conceal.

So great is the power of immigrationism that it causes liberals under its spell to pay lip service to what they otherwise despise, including acquisitiveness, material production, consumption, and economic individualism, and to praise immigrants who excel in pursuits that they condemn when native-born Americans succeed at them. (Since when do liberals otherwise measure personal worth by income, except inversely?) Similarly, immigrationism tempts conservatives to narrow *their* view until they can recognize only economic arguments and interests, becoming blind to traditional concerns that have historically defined conservatism. Since the Civil War and even before, liberal *and* conservative social critics have decried the rapacity, brutality, and vulgarity of an adolescent society bounding ahead unrestrainedly like Huckleberry Finn, always several lengths ahead of Miss Watson's civilizing grip.

Only when America slowed down, they argued; only when it was made to *stop moving,* to wash its face and hands, dress up, sit decorously in a straightback chair and study its lessons, could it become truly civilized, and thus take its place with the other civilized nations of the world. Civilization meant, among other things, a lessening of the crass desire to make money and a greater interest in art and learning, a slackening of the urge to sheer activity, and a desire for greater leisure. In the twentieth century, Herbert Croly, Jerome Frank, Bob Lafollette, Rexford Tugwell, as well as, more recently, William Appleman Williams, believed that the construction of a new republic depended upon limiting foreign entanglements and preventing the flow of labor and capital from abroad. Louis Adamic, the immigrant who helped to place Emma Lazarus's poem in the Statue of Liberty, wrote in *My America:* "Personally, I am against mass immigration, not because we already have millions of people unemployed, but for two other, I think more important, reasons. . . . America needs to give herself a chance, to take time to merge and integrate her population, study herself and determine what she really is, and gain some control over her cultural destiny." Today, mass immigration threatens to condemn the United States to endless cultural adolescence, robbing the nation of the prospect of a settling maturity.

The time is long overdue for America to emphasize conservation and consolidation over progression. Immigration, John Kennedy insisted, "infused the nation with a commitment to far horizons and new frontiers, and thereby kept the pioneer spirit of American life, the spirit of equality and of hope, always alive and strong." Alas, as Frederick Jackson Turner understood, when the physical frontier is gone, pioneering is gone also. Insofar as a consensus ever existed in favor of immigration early in the nineteenth century, it arose from agreement that immigrants were useful to the process of nation-building by fighting the Indians, settling the land, manning an industrializing economy, and setting the imprint of Western civilization indelibly upon the wilderness. By the 1890s, the United States had outgrown that (always fragile and uncertain) consensus. Lord Bryce in *The American Commonwealth* gave his American cousins a moving warning. "Gentlemen, why in heaven's name this haste? You have time enough. No enemy threatens you. No volcano will rise from beneath you. Why sacrifice the present to the future, fancying that you will be happier when your fields teem with wealth and your cities with people? In Europe we have cities wealthier and more populous than yours, and we are not happy. You dream of your posterity; but your posterity will look back to yours as the golden age. . . . Why, in your hurry to subdue and utilize Nature, squander her splendid gifts? Why hasten the advent of that threatening day when the vacant spaces on the continent shall all have been filled, and the poverty or discontent of the older states shall find no outlet?" Bryce, an English aristocrat, saw precisely what was "exceptional" about America, and also how Americans were bent on throwing that exceptionalism away.

Harry Truman thought that the dead hand of the past lay most heavily on America in respect of immigration. He was wrong: The hand he perceived was a living hand, an Invisible Hand moving immigrants across the ocean to the United States with rapid stealth. That is not to say that a supposed tradition of free immigration to America is anything but a myth. But even if it were historical fact, that would be no good reason not to challenge it. "As our case is new, so must we think and act anew. We must disenthrall ourselves," said Lincoln. "[T]he same elements that build up an institution eventually lead to its downfall," wrote Toynbee. "Immigration reform," Governor Lamm argues, "is not the death of the American Dream. . . . It is the necessary precondition for the preservation of the dream." The conscience of a child is not the same thing as the conscience of an adult. Neither are the responsibilities.

HERDER CALLED NATIONS IMAGES OF GOD. SOLZHENITSYN describes them as "the wealth of mankind; they are its generalized personalities; the smallest of them has its own particular colors and embodies a particular facet of God's design." Peter Brimelow insists that the nation be understood as a family, which Chesterton famously described as "a fighting thing, like a ship." Daniel Patrick Moynihan defines it as the largest aggregate of "people who *believe* they are ancestrally related." The United States being the richest, most powerful and influential member of the United Nations, one might suppose that the fact of its nationhood is as much accepted for granted as that of Great Britain, France, or Somalia. That is scarcely the case, however—in the United States, which Allan Bloom said was a system founded by philosophers and their students, a great stage on which political theories are personified. Bloom's view is shared by many other writers today, including Mark Falcoff, who believes that "[u]niquely among nations, America is a 'proposition country;' it has no history and identity apart from certain eighteenth-century political notions embodied in its Constitution and Common Law." Falcoff, who seems strangely unaware that the British Common Law embodies "notions" predating the eighteenth century by many foregoing ones, does not recognize that it also is of vastly greater importance to the American political tradition than the Constitution, which is unimaginable in theory and in practice without it. Even so, the propositionists' arguments are less remarkable for the thinness of their historical sense than they are for their determination to depersonalize the United States, by reducing it from an historical presence to an intellectual abstraction whose concrete reality is that of a democratic machine.

Attempts to abstract the American identity are discernible as early as the Progressive Era, when Herbert Croly wrote (in *The Promise of American Life*) that only a "democratic social ideal" could serve as the "ultimate bond of union" to sustain a highly differentiated society. Three decades later, Gunnar Myrdal (who was not after all an American) restated Croly's "ideal" comprehensively when he identified an "American Creed," defined by him as "the most explicitly expressed system of general ideals in reference to human interrelations" ever developed by a Western society. Arthur M. Schlesinger Jr. has praised the Creed for "facilitat[ing] the appeal from the actual to the ideal," without thinking to specify the ideal *what*. The ideal nation? Government? Society? Philosophy? The ideal religion? Does the American Creed point the way to Plato's Republic, Harvard University, or the Millennium?

The propositionists assert their claim for America's uniqueness in the history of the world by denying the American nation a coherent personality, the attribute most wholly unique to any human individual or group. This endeavor is congenial with that of the immigrationists—usually one and the same parties—who argue that the United States is special for being "a nation of immigrants." Of course all nations are nations of immigrants, or the descendants of immigrants. As Tom Paine reminded his countrymen, "The first king of England of the present line ... was a Frenchman, and half the peers of England are descendants from the same country." Every nation, representing the melding of ethnicity and culture, begins as a "cultural ingathering" which gradually evolves an ethnic identity. While America's racial homogeneity has been diluted by periodic influxes of immigrants and cultures, the process differs in degree, not in kind, from that by which other nations—including other Western nations—have developed.[15] Great Britain, Belgium, and Sweden have historically been receptive to immigrants, while Germany accepted the Huguenots in the seventeenth century and, after 1870, hundreds of thousands of Poles, to say nothing of millions of ethnic Germans from eastern Europe following World War II. Since the late nineteenth century, France has received several waves of immigrants; it formally welcomed immigrants after 1945, and declared itself an "emigration country" in the 1970s. From 1960 to 1973, western Europe absorbed some thirty million migrant workers and their families before the guest-worker program was shut down.[16] As Peter Brimelow has remarked, the chief difference between the United States and the great European nations is not the process that created them, but the vastly accelerated pace at which the formation of the American nation occurred. Reinhold Niebuhr decades ago criticized the dismissal by progressives of "the organic unities of family, race, and nation as irrational idiosyncracies which a more perfect rationality will destroy." Ben Wattenberg's "first universal nation" manifestly would be no nation at all, which is why the concept is so attractive, and also useful, to those who have an interest in denying that the United States is a nation in the traditional cultural, ethnic, and geopolitical sense of the term.

Schlesinger describes America not only as a multiethnic country from its inception but "an interweaving of separate ethnic strands into a new national design." In order to maintain these strands in harmony with one another, the new nation created "a brand-new national identity" through the cooperation of "individuals who, in forsaking old loyalties and joining to make new lives, melded away ethnic differences"—an identity of a kind that remains unforged in Canada. In making this argument Schlesinger leans heavily for support on Crèvecoeur, who denied that two-thirds of the poor immigrants arriving in the United States could be said to have had a country—as a man with an unfaithful and unforthcoming wife cannot be said to have a marriage—but claimed that the American social and legal system conferred on them for the first time a nationality in the true sense of the word. Like Tocqueville, he thought that immigrants became Americans by exercise of their new rights and responsibilities vested in them by the Declaration of Independence and the Constitution.

An immigration historian has described the American Revolution as a case of environment winning out over heredity. But, as Schlesinger admits, the majority of the inhabitants of all thirteen colonies were descended from Great Britain, and American culture in the colonial period was preponderantly British. "Providence," John Jay wrote in *The Federalist* No. 2 (as quoted in Part I, p. 28) "has been pleased to give this one connected country to one united people, a people descended from the same ancestors, speaking the same language, professing the same religion, attached to the same principles of government, very similar in their manners and customs...." And while Melville was stimulated by the thought that "You cannot spill a drop of American blood without spilling the blood of the whole world," Tocqueville refers to Americans as "Anglo-Americans" throughout *Democracy in America,* which is pervaded by the recognition that the Anglo-Saxon character of the American people, rather than their democratic principles, produces the happiness of their individual lives and the stability of their institutions. Tocqueville died in 1859, before the great sea change in the national character began—substantially as a result of immigration. Edward Luttwack denies that Americans, lacking a shared culture and ethnic solidarity, have anything to unite them beyond shared beliefs, of which "equality of opportunity in the pursuit of affluence" is the most important. It is certainly true that we have less of culture and solidarity than we once had—though more than we are likely to enjoy in future if the New Immigration of the 1980s and '90s continues. Nevertheless, at the end of the twentieth century the old WASP culture remains the only national culture worthy of the name; not solely on account of its primary and defining role in creating the country and the nation, but because it represents today the inherited culture of an elite, an informal aristocracy of talent, learning, and accomplishment incomparably superior to the proletarian and peasant cultures imported by the immigrant waves from the Civil War to the present. The influence of these unsophisticated cultures made possible the rise of the mass culture in the early part of this century that threatens to displace the traditional one; yet, to the extent that the one has not succeeded in displacing the other completely, a genuine American culture, partially intact, remains.

Lawrence Fuchs has suggested that, since we live in a world composed of nation-states, it is imperative that we decide what kind of a nation we want to be. Some say that, for the United States, nationhood of any sort is impossible. Alexander Aleinkoff, general counsel for the Immigration and Naturalization Service, thinks that in its application to the U.S. the phrase "national community" is either an oxymoron or the product of wishful thinking, the country having progressed in diversity far beyond the mutual obligations that community presupposes. Others have argued that while the communitarian position has merit, it postulates subnational groupings that fail comprehensively to describe the reality of modern nation-states. But even if their assessment is accurate, why continue to compound confusion with confusion, thus making a bad situation worse? "Nations," Ben Wattenberg says, "are only people." How wrong he is.

The question is whether the United States has the will to enforce its laws, control its borders, and protect its identity, along with other interests. So far it self-evidently has lacked that will, though the possibility remains that it will one day rediscover it. Before it can do so, however, it will need to renovate the national conscience by revising the complicated moral drama presented by its immigration crisis. Eugene McCarthy argues that, by the classic definition of "colony" ("the arrival of large numbers of people who impose their cultural values on the pre-existing society"), the United States has become "a colony of the world." The United States, he says, is distinguished from other colonized nations solely by its refusal to use its considerable power to prevent the process from occurring. Westerners in general, and Americans in particular, are agreed that colonialism is immoral. So why is colonization of Africa and Asia unconscionable, but colonization of North America a moral imperative? The proposition is on the order of saying that while murder is criminal, suicide is something to be encouraged.

A contributor to *Forum* magazine in 1892 remarked that "it seems almost pusillanimous to refuse a refuge to the oppressed and to the industrious and capable of other lands for fear that the institutions of this country may suffer." In 1923, a writer for the *North American Review,* admitting that "Those who deny freedom to others, deserve it not for themselves and under a just God cannot long retain it," nevertheless concluded, "Our civilization is complicated enough and full of obscure pitfalls of misunderstanding to make us wary about introducing any more unassimilable elements than we can help."[17] In the 1990s the American public class disagrees on whether the United States, a wealthy and still relatively free nation in a world of mostly poverty-stricken and tyrannical ones, can justify restricting substantially its now generous immigration policy. Those who say it cannot tend to argue from individualist, personalist, and sentimental assumptions; those who disagree usually work from communitarian, corporatist, and prudential ones. This broader or more inclusive view is not wholly lost on their opponents, who frequently apply it to the sending countries: Kenneth Roberts, the author of *Northwest Passage* and other popular works of historical fiction, complained in 1918 that in respect of the immigration question, Americans had considered the rights of every nationality in the world except their own. Immigrationists balk, however, at the suggestion that the United States has a right, not to mention a duty, to attempt at least to manage the increase of its population, to determine the ethnic and racial composition of the people a half-century hence, and to ensure the stability of its social and political institutions in the foreseeable future.

Traditional republican theorists held that nations are subject to unbreakable cycles of growth and decay. Will Durant expressed this idea when he wrote that civilization begins in the consolidation of order, develops with the growth of liberty, and perishes through the coming of chaos. It is possible that America's concern with immigration at the turn of the last century was a partial expression of the submerged fear that the United States might not after all be exempt from what Brooks Adams called "the law of civilization and decay." Between the last *fin de siècle* and the present one, similarities of condition exist. Then as now, the United States was experiencing economic consolidation and the proletarianization of the working class, developments from which a greater international presence— soldiers, diplomats, and warships going out; immigrants coming in—provided distraction. "[L]ike the hordes of old, [the immigrants] are destined to conquer us in the end," an observer warned in 1923, "unless by some miracle of human controversy we conquer them first." Contemporary Americans have been trained not to contemplate the differences between the human races; is it still possible for them to recognize the age-old distinction between civilized and barbarous peoples? Whether or not the federal government should be in the business of promoting "culture," it ought certainly to be striving to protect civilization—which, at this time, it manifestly is not doing.[18]

The thesis of Peter Brimelow's *Alien Nation* is that immigration is a far greater threat to American public order than most Americans care to think about. In the same vein, Ira Mehlman of FAIR warns that future threats to the United States will come not from reconstituted evil empires, but instead from "billions of desperate people with no stake in and respect for the order our civilization has so meticulously established." The quickest and surest way to destroy the American nation is to treat it as something other than the nation it is, just as the most effective way to wreck what remains of global order is to treat the system of integral nation-states as something else than what *it* is. If I own a horse, that horse will not survive long if, under the delusion that it is a unicorn, I insist on giving it stardust to eat and moonbeams to drink. From the nationalist as well as the internationalist perspective, the final argument against mass immigration is CHAOS, the subject of a bit of anonymous English verse:

> Keep order in space
> And order in time,
> For disorder is chaos,
> And chaos is crime.

PLAYING GOD IN YELLOWSTONE IS THE INSPIRED TITLE OF a book by Alston Chase about federal mismanagement of the ecosystem of Yellowstone National Park, which resulted in the forest fires of 1988. Chase's subject is the inability of men, including men organized as government, to understand, foresee, plan, and manage as God understands, foresees, plans, and manages: an insight that applies to the human governance of nations as it does to that of parks. *Playing God in the United States* is the title of a book yet to be written describing the efforts of the managerial class to manage the United States as God might manage it, monitoring rogue comets, falling sparrows, and everything else in between. If such a book is ever conceived, the author may discover designer immigration to be among the New Class's more godlike conceptions, perhaps even its most ambitious one.

Unfortunately, the God that the New Class apes (or aims to replace) is the offended God of the antediluvian chapters of the Old Testament, fixing the present Creation with a vengeful eye. The difference between God and the New Class is that He made the world and it didn't, and that even in His wrath He loves the object of His anger, while the New Class has no such love. What Joseph Sobran calls "the alienated state" cordially despises its subjects, in respect of whom the conscience of the state and its apologists has become an inverted one. That is to say, as its sympathy and loyalty toward its fellow countrymen become more attenuated, it transfers them to foreign cultures and peoples. That self-interest lies behind this perverse attitude makes it more reprehensible yet.

The New Class is not necessarily shorthand for liberals and the sort of people whom Spiro Agnew disliked. Agnew himself is a member in good standing of that class, as the newest marble bust in the Capitol demonstrates. So is Ronald Reagan, who assured a Labor Day crowd at Liberty State Park in New Jersey, "I want more than anything I have ever wanted to have an Administration that will, through its actions, at home and in the international arena, let millions of people know that Miss Liberty still lifts her lamp beside the golden door." And so is Elliot Abrams, who with Franklin S. Abrams has described the Immigration Act of 1965 as "the most humanitarian and the most sensible in our nation's history." Cant and buzzwords cut across political affiliations as they do the New Class itself, for whose members life is salt that has lost its savor if they cannot be insiders and, following that, insiders at the top. In order to remain there, they are eager to avoid the kind of unvetted opinions that would result in their being hurled like rebellious angels into oblivion. As John Ney explains with grim amusement, "it is not so much that positions are supported as that negatives are avoided. Unchecked immigration has to be allowed because the alternatives are worse. Stopping such immigration could lead to a bad world image, to very bad 'relations' with Mexico and the rest of Latin America, and a shortage of menial labor ... and these negatives could trigger the biggest negative of all: stock market repercussions which could damage everyone's portfolio! So unchecked immigration must be allowed. Once such a decision is made, the full propaganda storm is unleashed, and we end up with glowing articles in *Time* (and everywhere else), and [people] demanding 'enrichment' and 'cultural diversity.'"[19]

Peter Brimelow emphasizes repeatedly in his work that the New Class hates the nation-state for the same reason that it loathes the free market: Both are systems that operate perfectly well on their own without the intervention of scores of thousands of eminently visible, to say nothing of well-paid, hands. That aside, there are many reasons why immigration is for the managerial class "manna from heaven," in Brimelow's phrase. Immigration gives it an excuse to congratulate itself on the moral superiority of its own xenophilia as it contrasts with the xenophobia of the lumpen majority, but the social and political problems and frictions it produces offer the pretext for further interventions in the private sphere by central, state, and municipal government.[20] To the extent that the federal government and its agencies have attempted to curb immigration, whether legal or illegal, their efforts have been chiefly devoted to preventing or assuaging "abuses" that might goad the American public to demand a halt to immigration altogether. Alan C. Nelson, then commissioner of the INS, told the Commonwealth Club in San Francisco that "our immigrant heritage" is one of our most important national institutions. However, he cautioned, the activities of groups such as Sanctuary endanger its future by risking a backlash "far more restrictive than any proposed in the past." (That great beast of an American public out there.) Six years later, his successor as commissioner, Doris Meissner, spoke with arresting candor for someone in her position: "We are being transformed," she said, all smiles in her voice. The research foundations, conservative as well as liberal and libertarian, are mostly immigrationist—in particular the Ford Foundation, one of whose reports ("Changing Relations: Newcomers and Established Residents in U.S. Communities," 1987) seemed to be saying that even if America's problems could be ameliorated by curtailing immigration, a restrictionist policy would relieve Americans of their obligation to confront their racism and xenophobia, and transcend them. A study by the Rand Corporation in 1993, having determined that the growing number of immigrant children in the United States was destroying the school systems of many major American cities, advocated the creation of bigger and more comprehensive federal programs to deal with the crisis. In the opinion of the Ford Foundation, "Immigration presents the nation with a challenge to interpret democracy both as a political doctrine and as a social and economic creed." Americans may suffer from "compassion fatigue," as Governor Lamm suggests; not so their political leaders and opinion makers, who show every symptom of "aggravated compassion." And not so what Gerda Bikales calls "the humanitarian establishment"—church leaders, secular humanitarians, providers of social and other welfare services; also, of course, immigration lawyers. The State Department cooperates by stretching a refugee and asylum policy that was originally designed to cope with occasional crises into an increasingly elastic master plan intended to respond to a permanent condition of international dislocation.[21] The New Class is antirural, anti-Christian, and it loathes American culture. Why shouldn't it love immigration?

American politicians are fond of remarking that immigrants are good for the United States because they are willing to "take risks," the implication being that Americans are *un*willing to do the same. In fact, the Americans least prepared to incur risk of any kind are the politicians themselves, which is a major reason why the United States effectively lacks an immigration policy. As one INS agent said in the 1980s, "Immigration enforcement is like being in a football game without a home team." Since the 1960s Congress has many times "reformed" the immigration system, the net result of its activity being to permit more immigrants to enter the United States with each succeeding change. David Simcox observes that if the Federal Reserve were managed the way immigration policy is managed, the board would respond to hyperinflation by expanding the money supply; it would base interest rates on "numbers and assumptions set in stone in 1965 and 1990"; and grant preferential interest rates to the relatives and children of those to whom it made loans in the last thirty years. ("But then money, unlike the welfare of American citizens, is something the federal government really cares about.") Early in the 1980s, the national government was content to leave its southern and northern borders to the protection of a Border Patrol with fewer officers than the New York City Transit Police had. So far as it is concerned, massive population growth produced in the future by immigration is unavoidable, and government's sole responsibility in the crisis is to "manage" the explosion in numbers.[22] In the face of massive public disapproval, Congress passed the amnesty provisions of the Immigration Reform and Control Act of 1986 as a response to pressure from Hispanic organizations, the liberal wing of the American Catholic Church, and the media. In an unexpected burst of patriotism, the INS opened 107 "legalization centers" across the United States on the great American holiday, Cinco de Mayo.

The Republican Party has so far shown hardly, if any, more interest in immigration control than have the Democrats. One reason is the notorious timidity of me-too Republicanism, reinforced by the fear that to oppose the arrival of largely nonwhite immigrants in the United States would be to enhance its country-club image. Even more important, perhaps, is the reluctance of the party's leaders to go against supply-side ideology, which denies that America is subject to limits, and the Reaganauts' happy-talk about it being always morning in America. Though Senator Alan Simpson led the Republicans to press, however reluctantly, for immigration "reform" in the 1980s, Simpson's concern has always been—until recently, at least—for blocking *illegal* immigration, while preserving the ceiling for legal immigrants at a high level. Jack Kemp is an ardent immigrationist; so is Phil Gramm; and so is William Bennett, for whom the immigration issue presents endless opportunities for the lavish public display of his book of personal virtues. With the exception of Pat Buchanan, most Republicans of national visibility have refrained from criticizing "reform," while taking care not to endorse it publicly, either: Pete Wilson's aides were saying as late as 1994 that they had never heard the governor criticize legal immigration.[23]

As for the Democratic Party, Clinton and Gore have displayed antagonism veiled only thinly as uninterest in the question of immigration, ignoring the recommendations of the Jordan Commission and giving every sign of sympathizing with Commissioner Meissner, while promising to reinforce the Border Patrol. Perhaps the Clinton administration, which committed itself to paying special attention to problems relating to the economy, the environment, and education, has not noticed that these areas of public concern are among those worst affected by immigration. In 1989, the Census Bureau estimated that by 2050 the population of the United States would have risen to 303 million, a figure it revised upward in 1992 to 330 million, of which the historical ethnic majority would by then have become the largest minority population. The government, indeed, knows what is going on. ("We are being transformed.") Meanwhile, many state and local politicians, including Republican Mayor Rudolph Giuliani of New York City, encouraged by the attitude prevailing at the federal level, are declining to cooperate with the national government's laws for immigration control, arguing that it is not their job to enforce federal legislation. These, however, are never heard to complain that Washington should be doing a better job itself. "If you come here," Giuliani has said, "and you work hard and you happen to be in an undocumented state, you're one of the people we want in this city."

Those who talk about wishing to see America "strengthened" by immigration are all too often the same people who have succeeded in weakening it substantially in the past thirty years, and who apparently hope to weaken it still further in the future, wielding immigration as their most powerful weapon. "It is curious to me," Otis Graham reflects, "to find so many individuals of self-professed radical sentiments who choose to continue to offer an escape valve which harms the American lower classes and puts off the necessity in Mexico for facing the tragic inequalities in opportunity and the lack of social progress which characterizes recent Mexican history." Here perhaps Graham is being disingenuous. The parties to whom he refers view the white American working class (the "lower classes") as a counterrevolutionary lumpen bourgeoisie—a "labor aristocracy," in William Hawkins's phrase—*deserving* of harm, and the peons of Mexico and the other Third World countries as a lever by which native white American workers can be displaced and their masters overthrown. *Political Affairs,* the journal of the Communist Party U.S.A., asserts that "undocumented workers in any work . . . have the effect of depressing wages and lowering the quality of working conditions," while the Marxist theoretician Mike Davis envisions "a black and Hispanic working class, fifty million strong. This is a nation within a nation, society within a society, that alone possesses the numerical and positional strength to undermine the American empire from within." Robert Rubin, a member of the National

Lawyers Guild and also of the Refugee Rights Project for the San Francisco Lawyers Committee for Urban Affairs (funded by the Ford Foundation), wrote in his contribution to the 1986 World Refugee Survey (funded by the U.S. Committee for Refugees, funded by Ford): "Naturalization, enfranchisement, petitioning for immigration of relatives, and political empowerment are the immediate tasks.... The Southeast Asians, Mexicans, and recently hundreds of thousands of Central American refugees must unite now for opposing immigration reform and English-language laws, and later for more important political objectives." Jim Corbett, known as the founder of the Sanctuary movement, in discussing Sanctuary's ulterior aims has described a process of what he calls "social jujitsu," which is to be accomplished by nonviolent insurgency provoked by government reaction, itself encouraged by the activities of immigrants passed along by the underground railroad based in Tucson.[24] According to Nathan Glazer, recently arrived immigrants constituted the vast majority of the membership of the Communist Party in the United States, giving rise to a saying among organizers for the CPUSA that "Whenever an American joins the Party there is open opposition that he is a spy." Glazer's guess is that not more than one in ten of its members was a native-born American.[25]

In the climate of moral relativism that pervades contemporary America, where mere claim of conscience is sufficient to establish the claimant's bona fides, it is easy to forget that the word "conscience" is best thought of as a phrase fragment: that there are, in other words, bad consciences as well as good consciences, and that it is a paramount duty of societies, as well as of individuals, to distinguish between them.

—

ENTHUSIASTS FOR MULTICULTURALISM SEEM TO THINK THAT
it is a recent invention of the American Association of University Professors, perhaps inspired by that fad of the 1970s, the
block party. In fact, multiculturalism is nearly as old as human
history itself, though only in the last few thousand years has it
achieved its fullest realization as a world community of nations.
In modern times, the international order of nation-states *is*
multiculturalism. "Paradoxical though it may seem," Diane
Ravitch says, "the United States has a common culture that is
multicultural." Her statement is by no means paradoxical: It is,
quite simply, wrong. As John Lukacs has pointed out, when
people speak of "multicultural" they really mean "multicivilizational," indicating the coexistence of utterly different civilizations within a single country—which is a manifest impossibility. Leon Bouvier, a restrictionist who is also a political and
social liberal, emphasizes that his opposition to immigration is
demographic rather than cultural when he claims that "Fifty
million people of different racial and ethnic backgrounds living
harmoniously together [in California] would be the ultimate
model of a 'true community' for the rest of the world." However, the majority of his fellow anti-immigrationists are far less
sanguine about what one of them refers to as "the new
Moslemo-Santerio-Buddho-Confucio-Judeo-Christian society."[26] While a vote of Congress could alter *E pluribus unum* to
E pluribus multum, the only true "multicultural experience"
awaits us only in Heaven (or Elsewhere).

James Fallows discovers "the glory of American society" in "its
melding of many peoples," and Ben Wattenberg rejoices that

"In America, we now come from everywhere, getting along pretty well with each other, and vastly enriched by our pluralism." "One of the nicer effects" of immigration, Julian Simon adds, "is that it increases cultural variety." Why America, with a quarter of a billion people from "everywhere," requires still more "diversity" the immigrationists never explain, nor do they appear to have considered whether the emigration of tens of millions of the American lower classes to the nations of western Europe, Argentina, South Africa, Japan, Canada, and Mexico would "enrich" the receiving countries.

From the colonial period until now, proponents of immigration have argued that immigrants, being harder-working and more intellectually vigorous than the American native-born, substantially revitalize our institutions. This argument has lately been revised to suggest that the Western political heritage will be better defended by Third World immigrants than by the descendants of the nation's original stock. "It is the converts to a tradition who bring the most imagination and vigor to its defense," Lawrence A. Uzzell of the Hoover Institution believes. "A tradition especially needs newcomers to stir things up when it gets so decayed that the challenge is not to conserve but to restore." Uzzell finds the "boisterous" Hispanic immigrants of today reminiscent of the Scots-Irish immigrants in the eighteenth century, who pushed through the genteel English civilization of the tidewater region to the western frontier: "The tax revolts and anti-euthanasia protests of the 21rst century will need them." Richard Rodriguez speculates that Americans who believe that America has an immigration problem have got the situation backward. "No one wonders if perhaps America has a native-born problem. Does America need the native-born?"

Everyone concedes that immigrants do not come here for the *purpose* of accomplishing this massive task of historical and moral renovation, and that their interest in the United States is predominantly materialist and opportunistic. But very many have not considered whether the United States is more likely to achieve a moral, cultural, and political renaissance by the importation of alien cultures than by an honest process of self-reformation, nor have they examined the value of "variety." Finally, the assumption that multiculturalism offers an almost infinite array of possibilities has gone unchallenged, though in fact it is *not* the choice to end all choices, a resolution and a solution to the nation's problems, the freedom whereby to delimit every freedom: rather, multiculturalism precludes *another* set of options and ideals, among them the preservation of America as we know it.

The unquestioned—and unquestioning—power of the multiculturalist standard is in some degree the power of a pseudo-religious impulse. As early as the 1920s, Julius Drachsler wrote of "the will of America to become a truly spiritual nationality"—a reformulation in religious terms of what others attacked as "mongrelization." Drachsler's idea is the seed of the multiculturalist oak, a first brick in a new Tower of Babel said to be not only acceptable to but demanded by God, the first step toward a re-created Garden of Eden where the Celt and the Ethiope lie down together. At one level of understanding, multiculturalism is the ultimate religious vision of the most thoroughly secularized society in the history of the world.

At another level, it is something quite different. For almost a century before 1965, waves of immigration carried to the United States scores of millions of people who differed racially, ethnically, culturally, and religiously from the native stock to which they assimilated imperfectly, under a degree of duress, and with a grace that was partially feigned. Like a western river that emerges from the desert hardpan, flows above ground for miles, and sinks once more below the surface of the ground, their resentment has risen and fallen throughout the succeeding generations, emerging most visibly in the early 1970s with the "rise of the unmeltable ethnics" announced by Michael Novak less than a decade after the Immigration Act of 1965. It is owing to this resentment that the multiculturalists' slogans have so often been exercises in evasion, distractions from their deepest-lying motives and concerns. Julian Simon accuses restrictionists of employing a secondary concern for

values and institutions as a hypocritical cover for racist prejudices that are unacceptable in public discourse at the end of the
twentieth century. It does not occur to him that this weapon of
attack is a double-edged sword, multiculturalism being a form
of alienism and of reverse racism as well. In part a legacy of the
New Left of the 1960s, it is a Trojan Horse whose intended
function is the "transformation" of the United States by the
demotion and perhaps even the destruction of the old WASP
culture, driven by simple loathing disguised as academic theory
and a political agendum.

This loathing, frequently expressed by ill-contained glee, is
pervasive in discussions of Third World immigration and multiculturalism, often in the form of descriptive statement.
"Without fully realizing it, we have left the time when the nonwhite, non-Western part of our population could be expected to
assimilate to the dominant majority. In the future, the majority
will have to do some assimilation of its own." (Martha
Farnsworth Riche, *Time*.) "In its Third Century, American culture may no longer be based predominantly on European
themes. Its motifs may be as much Latin or Asian as traditional
Anglo-American." (Joel Kotkin and Yoriko Kishimoto, *The
Third Century*.) In *The First Universal Nation* Ben Wattenberg
enthuses that five of the seven top American tennis players in
1989 were children of immigrants or minorities, and asks if
tennis may not be a metaphor, and five out of seven "a portrait
of the future?" A series of articles published as "The Disap-
pearing Border" by *U.S. News and World Report* in 1985
described illegal immigrants as "the heirs of Cortes and Coro-
nado," reclaiming the land their forebears "took from the Indians and lost to the Americans. . . . an invasion and a revolt." In
1986 Robert Reinhold of the *New York Times* concluded an article entitled "Flow of Third World Immigrants Alters Weave of
U.S. Society" with the sentence, "It may be the last laugh will
be had by the last Mexican Governor of California, who report-
edly said in 1847: 'We find ourselves suddenly threatened by
hordes of Yankee emigrants whose progress we cannot arrest.'"
A. M. Rosenthal, in his column for the same paper some years
ago, strikingly described his experience with the Border Patrol

on the Texas side of the international line. "Slithering along in the dark, I suddenly thought, I'm one too—a wetback, and so was my father. . . . 'Davey,' I was finally able to whisper, to my fellow editor, 'I am one of them,' pointing across the river. 'Not one of them,' pointing to the young men of the Border Patrol." Significantly, the two ethnic American groups historically most resentful of WASP dominance collaborated to bring about immigration reform in 1965. Senator Kennedy's *A Nation of Immigrants* was published in its first edition in 1958 by the Anti-Defamation League of the B'nai B'rith, which blamed the United States's immigration policy in the 1930s for the deaths of hundreds of thousands if not millions of Jews in the Holocaust, and hoped for a more generous reception by America of world Jewry in future.

Whatever the motive, the immigration enthusiasts' commitment to multiculturalism is fervid enough to cause them to subordinate to it the welfare of America's "first minority." Liberal (and other) apologists for immigration show elaborate uninterest when confronted—as President Clinton was by a black youth on a visit to Los Angeles in the wake of the race riots in 1992—by arguments that large numbers of unskilled immigrants displace native blacks on the job market. Anthony Maingot suggests that while the American Creed acknowledges the moral claims of both American blacks and immigrants, the absence of historical guilt in respect of the immigrants gives blacks, as between the two groups, the moral edge. Increasingly, however, this seems not to be the case. Vernon Briggs calls present immigration policy "a revived instrument of institutional racism," whether intended as such or not. "It provides a way to bypass the national imperative to address the employment, job preparation and housing needs of much of the urban black population." In the opinion of Ron Unz, a California entrepreneur and Republican politician, blacks are socially far more disruptive than immigrants, and their own worst enemies; therefore, he implies, we should not make immigrants a scapegoat on their behalf. (Unz's comment—recalling a statement in the *Mobile Register* in 1900 that "a million active Chinese in the South [are wanted] to wake the negro population into activity"—was answered by the editors who had printed his article with the tart observation that American blacks *are* nevertheless Americans, unlike the illegal immigrant population of San Jose.) As for the country's Native Americans, the immigrationists seem never to have given them a thought, although the tribes of the Southwest in particular are vulnerable to hordes of job and welfare seekers from across the border, with whom they are in competition for public monies and other aid. The Maori of New Zealand have deplored that country's switch from a bicultural to a multicultural perspective, but no one in America knows what the tribes think about continued mass immigration. Their opinion is never solicited, probably because no one cares to know it. Even environmentalists appear not to have considered the subject. One thinks of the teary-eyed Indian on the poster dreamed up years ago for the antilitter campaign. How does *he* feel about the trashing of his homeland by tens of millions more immigrants? (The ad campaign we'll never see.)

"There's only room for one minority in this town" is an oft-repeated maxim following the riots in Los Angeles. Whether or not that is so, numerous studies have shown that immigrants have had damaging effects on the welfare of the indigenous black population. Bruce Porter and Marvin Dunn (in *The Miami Riots of 1980*) present statistics indicating job displacement by the mostly Cuban immigrants, and cite complaints of black businessmen that capital available from the federal government for minority enterprises went to Hispanics rather than to blacks. "They bring everybody to Miami: Nicaraguans, Cubans, Haitians," one black rioter said during the Mariel boatlift. "And we're still on the bottom."[27] Two years later, the Center for Immigration Studies found that the 1965 Immigration Act, by providing employers with an alternative labor supply, largely negated the economic potential of the Civil Rights Act of the previous year. In the 1970s, the Rockefeller Commission on population growth warned that the effects that immigration was having on native racial and ethnic minorities required careful scrutiny. Frank Morris, dean of graduate studies and urban research at Morgan State University and a member of the board of directors at CIS, testified before the House Sub-committee on Immigration, Refugees, and International Law in 1990 that immigrants, in addition to taking blacks' jobs, barred them from other work by the creation of language barriers and exacerbated the crisis in urban education. (The committee seemed little interested in his remarks.) And William Frey of the University of Michigan has done demographic research suggesting that immigrants push poor blacks out of formerly black metropolitan areas, beyond which they have no prospects.

As early as the seventeenth century blacks in America have resented immigrants, who outpaced them rapidly in economic and social progress. Frederick Douglass said, "Every hour sees the [free] black man elbowed out of employment by some newly arrived immigrant whose hunger and whose color we thought to give him a better title to the place." In a famous address delivered at the Atlanta Exposition in 1895, Booker T. Washington exhorted American industrialists to "Cast down your buckets where you are"—by which he meant to say, Hire the freedmen and their descendants in your factories, do not import millions of immigrants to do the work. (Washington believed that the Chinese lacked moral standards and were unassimilable to Western civilization.) In the early decades of the twentieth century, Afro-American politicians warned that Greek and Italian immigrants would take jobs from blacks, and the majority of black leaders favored restriction after World War I and in the 1920s, when the Pullman Company hired Filipinos to thwart the efforts of A. Philip Randolph to organize black railroad workers. Native blacks historically have resented even black immigrants from the British West Indies, who began arriving in substantial numbers in the 1890s, and from Haiti. Peter Skerry thinks that "this conclusion doesn't carry with it any clear prescription for immigration. Blacks continue to have a strong claim on America's conscience. Yet this doesn't necessarily point to restrictionist policies." One wonders why not, for a society that refuses to take chances with nonregulation car seats for children and unapproved food additives. If there is so much as a suspicion that immigrants harm the American black population, why accept the risk by permitting mass immigration of unskilled workers to continue?

A good reason is the obsession that influential elements of American society have with multiculturalism. Another is the ambition of American politicians, ethnic ones in particular, for whom multiculturalism, in combination with immigrationism, offers irresistible opportunities. A Roper survey in 1990 indicated that 74 percent of Hispanic Americans opposed increased immigration quotas; according to Skerry, 47 percent of blacks in California, and an even greater percentage in south-central Los Angeles—substantially a Latino community—supported Proposition 187. In the face of widespread suspicion of immigration on the part of American blacks and Mexican-Americans and the desire of both communities that it be reduced, black and Mexican-American "leaders"—almost all of them Democrats—promote continuing mass immigration as a means of furthering broader political and social agenda in which, supposedly, their constituencies have a shared interest. During the debates on Simpson-Mazzoli, the Congressional Black Caucus opposed employer sanctions and regularly supported the Hispanic Caucus on other immigration-related issues. Jesse Jackson in his presidential bid was expected by many to adopt a restrictionist stand on immigration; instead, he joined with "spokesmen" for the Mexican-American population and denounced Simpson-Mazzoli as racist as well as restrictionist—a position in which the entire Black Caucus, which identified employer sanctions as a civil rights issue, joined him. (If passed, Jackson warned, Simpson-Mazzoli would require Americans to carry identification passbooks as South Africans do, while "No Latino will ever be able to go to work or take a walk without the threat of harassment, arrest, or even deportation.") Throughout the Democratic primary, Jackson was the only one of three candidates to oppose Simpson-Mazzoli *and* to insist upon an open-borders plank. His militancy on the issue pushed Walter Mondale, in a debate with Gary Hart and Jackson in Grapevine, Texas, to warn that Simpson-Mazzoli would lead to identification cards, a threat to Hispanics' civil rights, and a "big roundup" of illegals. A comment by

Sheila Graham, the national coordinator for Jackson's Rainbow Coalition, suggests what black and Hispanic politicians have in mind with regard to immigration. "If current immigration and birthrates continue, by the year 2000, Latinos will be the largest ethnic group in the United States. Since 85 percent of all Spanish-speaking people are concentrated in nine states and twenty cities that control 193 (or 71 percent) of the electoral votes needed to win the Presidency, they constitute a critical swing vote in future elections."[28]

Unlike immigrationists, doctrinaire multiculturalists are exclusively political and cultural liberals. Since liberalism, in spirit as in doctrine, points not to multiculturalism but to uniculturalism, there appears to be a contradiction here. Liberals tend toward universalism, and universalists want people all over the world to surrender their cultural peculiarities and even identities, as Allan Bloom argued that Americans must do when confronted by multifarious immigrations at home. "Diversity," as Lasch has noted, "affronts their vision of the unity of all mankind." So the question is, Why are not the proponents of multiculturalism promoting uniculturalism instead?

The answer seems to be that for liberals multiculturalism is the next best thing to uniculturalism: the only means in sight to prevent one culture—for white liberals, their own—from continuing to "dominate" other cultures, a situation they regard as "illiberal." (It is probably not coincidental that President Johnson, in signing the Immigration Act of 1965, looked forward to "a world where no country rules another. . . .") An obvious way to combat and, eventually, to destroy the hegemony of the dominant cultural influence is to deny that an identifiable culture constitutes the magnetic core of a heterogeneous civilization— which is precisely the strategy of those who insist that America is a "proposition country" and a "universal nation." They protest overmuch. On the contrary, the United States *does* possess a fundamental character, which is that of a British culture modified to a truly unique culture by the frontier (a blend, essentially, of Russell Kirk's vision of America with Frederick Jackson Turner's), to which immigrants arriving after 1790 had at least in some degree to assimilate. (American "conservative" academicians and journalists who resist multicultural advances in the name of "Western civilization" apparently share with their liberal opponents the belief that an American civilization does not exist: a misunderstanding best explained by the impact of intellectual émigrés from Europe in the pre- and postwar periods, and their subsequent influence on American culture and the American academy.) Will Herberg, writing in the 1950s, observed that "the American's image of himself is still the Anglo-American ideal it was at the beginning of our independent existence. The 'national type' as ideal has always been, and remains, pretty well fixed. It is the *Mayflower,* John Smith, Davy Crockett, George Washington, and Abraham Lincoln that define America's self-image, and this is true whether the American in question is a descendant of the Pilgrims or the grandson of an immigrant from southeastern Europe." "So far as I know," Thomas Fleming claims, "I don't have a drop of real English blood in my veins . . . but insofar as I am an American, I am also English in the same way some tree-worshipping Celt or skull-swilling German had to become a Roman if he was to live within the empire. If we really are the last generation of Anglo-Americans, then we are also the last generation of Americans, period." Anna Quindlen, on the other hand, thinks the American nation is "a coast-to-coast contradiction, a country populated by a potpourri of onetime outsiders that has nevertheless harbored a deep-seated xenophobia"; an opinion that is lent academic solidity by David Bennett when he calls the nativists' suspicion of alien groups "always a paradox in the multiethnic, multiracial world of America. . . ." But if America really was multicultural, suspicion is not paradoxical; while, if it wasn't, Bennett's statement is meaningless.

One often hears in favor of multiculturalism the argument that it represents "the education of America." No one, however, explains why America is in need of education (meaning reeducation?) by other cultures, or why Americans should submit to the renovation of their own. Even Julian Simon has graciously acknowledged that "Wanting to maintain the human character of your country as it is, or has been, is not necessarily racism, nor is it necessarily illogical." Quite the contrary, you might say: Peter Skerry has suggested that there is something perverse about a country many of whose citizens believe otherwise. The immigrants themselves want to maintain their cultures here, or at least many of them do—a wish with which many Americans sympathize, as they sympathize with the desire of native Barbadians to protect their way of life against immigrants. Why then should we not wish to protect our own culture? There is no instance in history in which the dominant racial group within a modern industrial nation-state has permitted its place to be usurped by another, subordinate one. The submersion of American culture by another, or others, is of itself not necessarily a good thing, or a bad one. The issue is simply, Is it something that the American people wish to have happen?

It is beginning to be noticed that "secular uniformitarianism" as observed and practiced in the United States is incompatible with cultural pluralism—incompatible, at least, so far as cultural coherency and public peace of mind are concerned. Unlike Great Britain, which has introduced courses in Christianity in its state-run schools for the purpose of acquainting British students (many of them Hindus and Muslims) with this crucial aspect of history and culture (not of inculcating Christian faith), the United States cannot tolerate a logical inconsistency at odds with notions of uniformity, which derive from the French revolutionary tradition that—while foreign to the framers—represents a strand of political thought that has tended to harden with time, along with the national arteries. The United States is threatened less by a plurality of cultures and of languages than it is by a plurality of *moral* languages among which our relativistic assumptions—and laws—do not allow us to "discriminate," so that we are tempted to take refuge in the ever more convenient pretense that moral language itself does not exist.[29] "The defining concept of multiculturalism," says Lawrence Auster, "is that our society is a collection of equal cultures, from which it follows that America's dominant Western culture is illegitimate and must be dismantled or dramatically weakened." Replace "equal cultures" in that passage with "equal moral systems," and the underlying effect of multiculturalism becomes apparent. Given the degree to which a common commitment to a democratic ideal has helped to bind an ethnically heterogeneous nation together, this unifying ideal will become even more critical in future as America becomes still more heterogeneous. Multiculturalism, then, strengthens the concept of the United States as a political idea. But a political idea, no matter how good a one, is not the same thing as a moral system, a national conscience that can only evolve historically, through time and cultural development. An enhanced concept of America as a political ideal can only lead to the growing conviction that the solution to the myriad problems associated with immigration, multiculturalism, and every other problem facing the nation is indoctrination in the right political ideas—what Claes Ryn calls the civics-class understanding of national history.

The word "ethnocentrism" was coined in 1900 and given widespread currency by William Graham Sumner in *Folkways,* published in 1907. Its opposite, "ethnofugalism," was first suggested, to the best of my knowledge, by Garrett Hardin to signify what he described as "a romantic flight away from our own culture." The tendency—which can be traced at least as far back as the sixteenth century, when the early explorations of America were exciting Europeans' imaginations in respect of the indigenous populations, whom many in the Old World were prepared to accept as innocent primitives and noble savages living an Edenic existence uncorrupted by civilization—is nothing new in Western history. An openness to other cultures is probably the deepest source of the multiculturalist impulse in America: an inherited European peculiarity, not an African, Asian, or Latin American one. It may be that this anomalous characteristic of Western culture offers a partial solution to the mystery, recognized by almost every student of American immigration history, of how European-Americans could have permitted the movement of alien peoples to their shores, while deploring their arrival. The immediate one, however—as Auster argues in his perceptive book *The Path to National Suicide*—is the Immigration Act of 1965. Whether or not the authors of the act intended or imagined the ethnic transformation of the United States that it produced, the racial and cultural makeover that has occurred since "has insensibly led to acceptance of that transformation in the form of a new, multicultural vision of American society." Multiculturalism, Auster believes, is not a radical movement at all but a "mainstream phenomenon," the result of a demographic process leading predictably to a multiracial society. Simply, it is an attempt to make the best of a bad deal. Auster attributes not only multiculturalism but a shift in the attitude of the white majority toward the nonwhite minorities—call it tolerance or simply resignation—to the act of 1965. And indeed, as Nathan Glazer has remarked, nativist resistance to immigrants of alien cultures, languages, and religions has never been weaker. For restrictionists like Auster and the syndicated columnist Samuel Francis, the connection between multiculturalism and immigration is added reason for a less generous immigration policy. For immigrationists as a group, who see (or anyway profess to see) immigration as a type of natural phenomenon, the influx of aliens cannot be resisted, but only coped with. "We are rapidly creating, in the United States," Rushworth M. Kidder wrote in the *Christian Science Monitor,* "a truly multiracial society. The question is not whether to resist it or fight to promote it. The question for the future is how to manage it."

Apologists for immigration believe that little management is required in any case. "In an age of global television and the universality of American culture," Senator Edward Kennedy asserted on the Senate floor in 1965, "their assimilation, in a real sense, begins before [the immigrants] come here." More than thirty years earlier, a writer for the *Saturday Evening Post* had dismissed this superficial view of acculturation ("As a people, we foolishly thought we could Americanize them by dressing them in American clothes"), and ten years before that Henry Fairchild had warned that "Real assimilation means adoption into [our] spiritual inheritance." The current controversy regarding the education of immigrant children indicates that Fairchild's is the deeper and truer view. New York State's

"Curriculum of Inclusion," devised in the 1980s, was a direct response to changes produced in New York's population by immigration from countries of the Third World. Thomas Sobol, the state commissioner of education, explained: "The assimilationist ideal worked for ethnic peoples who were white but it is not working for ethnic people of color. Replacing the old, assimilationist view is a competing ethnic—cultural pluralism. Today we must accommodate not only a diversity of origins but a diversity of views." Several years later, a reporter for *Time* reflected that "Having embarked on the large-scale education of new immigrant children, the U.S. has no choice but to continue toward a distant if problematic future." Multiculturalism, in the schools as in society at large, in the 1990s is the social and moral equivalent of desegregation in the 1950s and '60s—the difference being that desegregation was an attempt to redress an inherited and unavoidable situation, while multiculturalism is supposed to be the solution for an avoidable, deliberately invited one. Perennial immigration is often presented as a chronic condition of American life, like black-white enmity, of which the United States cannot unburden itself. But why, if that is so, has the country failed to reach a moral consensus on the immigration question, as it has with the racial one?

Already in 1924, Kenneth Roberts observed in the *Saturday Evening Post* that "there has sprung up in America the conviction that lawmakers, public speakers and people who wish to preserve a reputation for fairmindedness must not openly say that certain races of people are less desirable material for future citizens of America than certain other races." But while restriction based on fears of mongrelization and theories of racial purity and superiority are fairly described as racist, there is no good reason to condemn as such objections to immigrants based on perceived racial and cultural incompatibilities. "I do not justify the brutality of the treatment of those Chinese who are here," James G. Blaine told the U.S. Senate in 1879, ". . . but you must deal with things as you find them. If you foresee a conflict upon that coast by reason of an immigration that calls for the interposition of the military, I think it is a good deal cheaper to avoid the trouble by preventing the immigration." In 1952 the Senate Judiciary Committee—under pressure from the executive branch to repeal the national origins system— asserted in its report that, while its members held no brief for claims of Anglo-Saxon superiority, they were nevertheless agreed that the Quota Law of 1924 had rationally and logically sought to preserve the sociological and demographic balance of the United States, whose original stock were morally justified in determining that their nation was no longer "a field for colonization." This line of argument, which today is almost totally unacceptable across the political spectrum, represents a considerable departure from the American founding myth, which Lawrence Fuchs has described as ideological rather than tribal, but implicitly racial nonetheless.[30]

Second only to sexual differentiation, the attribute of race most significantly separates one human being from another. John R. Commons, who believed that E pluribus unum had nothing to do with race and culture, understood the central task of the early American Republic to have been the unision of a scattered population, diverse in its experience of climate and enjoyment of resources, into a single self-governing nation; the important work of twentieth-century America, he thought, was to bring together as one people a multitude of races more variegated than the continent itself. In the end, however, multiculturalism, like feminism, is certain to be unsuccessful, and for a similar reason: Ethnic groups, like human females, are fundamentally mistrustful of one another and therefore incapable of sustaining the "solidarity" that their programs demand if they are to prevail. In Ben Wattenberg's opinion, races and ethnic groups in the United States get along pretty well, since geographical mobility has "scrambled most of our eggs together." Julian Simon calls it "a major blessing for the United States that it can accept large numbers of immigrants without having to worry about injecting an indigestible minority into a homogeneous majority," thanks to the nation's having overcome ethnic conflict long ago, and urges Americans not to let "the occasional appearance of racism or of opinion polls showing antagonism to immigrants fool us into thinking that public hostility [to immigration] is greater than it really is."

Yet both Schlesinger and Moynihan have recently predicted that ethnic and racial conflict is likely in future to succeed the ideological battles of the past. In reprimanding the American native majority for what he considered its churlish, ungenerous, and prejudiced response to earlier generations of immigrants, Fairchild felt in honesty compelled to deplore also the "even more bitter race prejudice existing between various foreign groups," which he recognized as another barrier to assimilation. The Irish settlers of California, for example, were fervent exclusionists in the 1880s. Fairchild tells a story about a New England lady escorting her son to be enrolled in the local public school and discovering that he was the only American child there. "A Russian Jewess edged up to her and remarked confidentially, 'Ain't it a shame, the way the Dagoes are crowding in everywhere these days?'" In 1983, Jan Luytes of Florida International University warned that displacement of blacks from their jobs by Cuban and Haitian émigrés had created considerable ethnic tension in Florida; a decade or so later, a Mason-Dixon poll indicated that 77 percent of non-Hispanic whites and 72 percent of non-Hispanic blacks thought that the quality of Floridian life had been damaged by immigration from Cuba, while 1 percent felt it had been improved by it. Native blacks have demonstrated hostility to blacks from Santo Domingo, Haiti, Jamaica, Nigeria, and Ethiopia, and the newcomers have been happy to return the favor. Moreover, signs of a response by whites to cultural and racial displacement have begun to appear. Richard D. Alba speculates that contemporary white ethnicity serves to unite all white Americans, and Glaister and Evelyn Elmer predict that the "biggest shocker" will be the commitment of formerly unassertive whites to the protracted ethnic wars. The Marxists and liberals at the end of the nineteenth century who believed that liberal and socialist ideals would efface ethnic self-consciousness have been proved wrong. "The United States," Moynihan warns, in almost Faulknerian language, ". . . will know more than it has known of grief. . . . We have known the grief of caste-imposed subjection; we must now expect caste retaliation." The radical but familiar division between black and white in America, he foresees, will be splintered by the complicating presence of immigrants of every race arrived in the country since the 1960s.

It is an imperative of every human culture to seek ascendancy over those others with which it is juxtaposed. The most dramatic example of cultural aggression and usurpation in the United States is Miami, where the "Anglos" have been displaced—culturally, linguistically, economically, and politically—by the "Hispanics," and the fact of their subordinate status is regularly impressed upon them by their successors. It may be true that immigrants do not intend to impose their cultures on the native population, but nevertheless they do so, when they can. Other times they *mean* takeover, directly and without apology. "Racism" itself is not a European invention; only the term for it is. Some liberals know this: Richard Reeves, noting that racism is a way of life in Asia and elsewhere, once remarked that he had never visited a country where the people were not racists, and James Fallows believes that racist societies are the norm throughout the world. Sociobiology has discovered ethnic and racial hostilities to be innate to the human species—an evolutionary mechanism—while historians have shown them to persist between groups over thousands of years, and also, within the confines of a single socially complex society, to replicate antagonisms between nations. The fond American belief that people will not jeopardize their economic well-being to the gratification of their ethnic and racial resentments ought to have been exploded long before now. "Americans tend to assume that ethnic conflict occurs only when one group is subordinate and another dominant and therefore will be eliminated with progress toward an unranked system. Again, experience elsewhere disproves this comforting belief. Most ethnic group relations in other countries are not between clearly superordinate and subordinate groups, but ethnic conflict is practically universal."[31]

In 1916, the year before the United States entered the Great War on the side of the Allies, John Commons warned that Americans had already begun to "despotize" their democratic institutions for the purpose of controlling "dissident elements" recently arrived from overseas. Immediately following the nation's commitment to the struggle, this process of despotization increased significantly, lasting well beyond the peacemaking and creating a legacy that civil libertarians have deplored ever since. While it is true that the "hyphenated-Americans" were generally not disloyal to their adoptive country during the war years, it is also the case that their presence was a worrisome and destabilizing element on the home front, and that immigrants were widely involved in radical and anti-American activities in the 1920s and '30s. Auster has commented on the paradox that a universalist order founded on a liberal understanding of individual rights should depend on America's remaining culturally particularist, identifiably one people. This argument is inadvertently endorsed by Richard Brookhiser, an editor for *National Review* and the author of an admiring book in defense of the White Anglo-Saxon Protestant and his culture, who is nevertheless an enthusiastic immigrationist. WASPs, according to Brookhiser, define themselves by citizenship rather than by class and extended family ties, including those of race and ethnicity. Hence, he argues, they have displayed a distaste for particularism ("Vendettas and blood feuds were considered the marks of yokels, while 'special interest' has long been a political term of abuse") and looked to their individual consciences when considering their duty in respect of the moral law. Though Brookhiser has chosen to overlook the caste-consciousness and social pride of White Anglo-Saxon Protestant society, he is right in remarking a universalist aspect in its social and political assumptions. But the problem for WASPs—and for the United States—is that, while they persist in their adherence to this strain of universalism, everyone else in America, and indeed the world, is becoming more self-consciously particularist. For this reason, there is cause to fear that non-European immigration may lead in time not just to radical changes in the composition of the American people, but to a dissolution of what remains of the laws and institutions they have enjoyed for centuries. Freedom, it begins to seem, may not be compatible with a multicultural society.

Commons perceived three foundations of a democracy: the intelligence of citizens, their "manliness," and "the capacity for cooperation, that willingness and ability to organize, to trust their leaders, to work together for a common interest and toward a common destiny, a capacity which we variously designate as patriotism, public spirit, or self-government." Western travelers in the Third World have noticed that "cooperation" especially is lacking among its peoples, who are typically unable or unwilling to look beyond family or clan. In accepting these as immigrants, does the United States risk becoming itself a Third World country—or no country at all—by a loss of community: not just ours, but *any* community? Leopold Tyrmand, the late Polish novelist and émigré, said that the United States is really *two* immigrant countries—the America of Plymouth Rock and the America of Ellis Island—and that the second owes its existence to the security of the first. Paradoxically again, *real* ethnocentrism is an about-to-be minority culture's belief that it can dominate a rising majority culture, or rather a congeries of minority cultures more or less united in opposition to the former majority one. Whereas multiculturalism *in theory* is a product of the European mind and culture, multiculturalism *in fact* would replace the European-American civic conscience with . . . something else, most probably civil strife: eruptions of ethnic hatred, bloodshed, and repression of the sort endemic to eastern Europe, Africa, Asia, Latin America, and the Caribbean. Multiculturalism as it can only be realized in history outside the international system is not culture at all but chaos: the death of that supercultural construct, civilization. It is not something to hope—much less work—for.

"YOU SHALL WELCOME THE STRANGER AS YOUR OWN" HAS
been the eleventh commandment in the eyes of the American
religious establishment since 1945 or thereabouts. While the
more liberal denominations and left-wing adherents of every
church were on the cutting edge of the movement that produced the Immigration Act of 1965 and subsequent expansion-
ist reforms, their more moderate brothers and sisters in Christ
have not lagged far behind. From V-E Day until now, religious
groups and institutions in the United States have worked in
partnership with the federal government to assist, admit, and
resettle refugees, émigrés, displaced persons, asylum seekers,
and garden-variety immigrants, as well as to amend and liber-
alize the laws pertaining to them. For a significant portion of
organized believers in the United States, the immigrationist
movement has been an extension of the civil rights movement,
in which they were also prominent. "Whatever you did not do
for one of the least of these, you did not do for me . . . " (Matt.
25:31–46). Roy Beck, a prominent Methodist layman in addition to being the Washington correspondent for the *Social Contract,* calls it a rule of thumb that the more liberal the Christian
denomination, the more likely that its spokesmen will give the
passage a literalist reading. Over the years, the liberal Protestant churches have adopted immigrationist positions on a long
list of immigration-related issues, with which the laity has been
substantially in disagreement. The discrepancy is inferable
from any number of polls taken over the last few decades, indicating that the great majority of the American people—90 percent of whom call themselves religious—favor restriction. But
a Gallup poll taken in 1992 yielded more precise findings,

including that Christians are more likely than secularized Americans to want immigration reduced; that two-thirds of all Christian Americans oppose liberalized immigration policies, compared with 5 percent who support more generous ones; and that no statistically significant difference of opinion exists between Protestants and the Roman Catholics whose coreligionists have benefited so greatly from immigration in the past. Jim Dorcy, senior government relations associate of FAIR, has accused religious leaders of abusing their influence with elected officials who personally determine policy related to such matters as immigration, population increase, and environmental protection.[32] Gerda Bikales, an English-language advocate, is more blunt. "Time and again," she charges, "the religious leadership has skilfully manipulated its prestige and moral influence, winning concessions on immigration in a process somewhat akin to moral blackmail."

Heedless of the views of the pewsitters, the hierarchy of the Roman Catholic Church in America arguably bears a greater responsibility for three decades of liberal immigration policy than does any other single denomination in the United States. "As other societal institutions get on the anti-immigrant bandwagon," the *National Catholic Register* boasted in the fall of 1994, "the Church comes out squarely on the immigrants' side." Church leaders have called for a domestic "pro-immigration movement," and Roger Cardinal Mahoney of Los Angeles has outlined a set of principles that he believes should guide immigration reform as it is being debated in California. That these will not be in agreement with the ideas of Governor Wilson and the sentiments of the electoral majority that passed Proposition 187 is absolutely certain. The National Conference of Catholic Bishops has opposed employer sanctions ("The Church must be the first to insist that love knows no borders"), while refusing either to support or to condemn Sanctuary. The Immigration and Citizenship Office of the Los Angeles Catholic Archdiocese operated the biggest private program engaged in registering illegal aliens offered amnesty by the Immigration Reform and Control Act in 1986, and Church leaders in Los Angeles, New York, and Chicago have announced that they will willingly and knowingly hire immigrants regardless of their status with the INS. In the 1980s, Father Paul B. Marx told a congregation in Buffalo, "I tell the Mexicans when I am down in Mexico to keep on having children, and then to take back what we took from them: California, Texas, Arizona, and then to take the rest of the country as well."

Archbishop Mahoney has directly challenged the 1986 law by helping Los Angeles to find jobs for undocumented workers. He explains: "If the question is between the right of the nation to control its borders and the right of a person to emigrate in order to seek safe haven from hunger or violence (or both), we believe that the first right must give way to the second." Father Richard Ryscavage, S.J., formerly the director of Migration and Refugee Services at the U.S. Catholic Conference, concurs with this position. "The great question of who has a right to come to this country and who has a right to decide that right is very interesting," according to Father William J. Davis, a Jesuit priest then codirector of the Christic Institute in Washington, D.C., and an organizer for Sanctuary. The Catholic Bishops of California "forcefully" opposed Proposition 187, urging citizens of the state to reject an initiative which, they claimed, would "make us fearful and hostile to the strangers in our midst" and imperil human rights. John Swenson, the present executive director of MRS, while admitting that nations have a moral right to control their borders, insists that they are obligated nevertheless to meet the human needs of immigrants once they have penetrated those borders by whatever means, legal or illegal. The Archbishop himself has stated that his first concern is for what will effectively promote the common good, and also for "persons who have little political power." He did not, however, identify the parties for whom that good is a common good, or explain why persons who do not belong to the state or national polity should be expected to have political power within either of them.

Where immigration is concerned, as with too many other social and political issues, the churches fail to heed the injunction given them by their Founder, that they serve as the leaven of this world, and not be leavened by it. This failure is an aspect of the Americanization of Christianity that has accompanied the growth of Americanism as a secular religion. For the Catholic Church in America, the process began in the early part of this century when its American-born leadership emphasized the primacy of freedom of conscience, the importance of lay activity and Church democracy, and the compatibility of these with the national democracy, and proudly proclaimed their accommodationist sympathies by calling themselves "Americanists." While Americanism, compounded by liberal modernism, has infected Protestantism even more strongly, it seems particularly sad that the Roman Catholic Church, which for two thousand years has produced thinkers and moralists capable of the most delicate and refined distinctions, should have lately allowed itself to be led into much clumsy, wrongheaded, and fundamentally coarse moral discussion, influenced by the vulgarity and sentimentalism of progressive clichés. The blame is not the West's alone, since Latin America's liberation theologians have had a particularly damaging effect on contemporary moral theology. In the opinion of David Simcox (himself a Roman Catholic), liberation theology's "referential option for the poor" has tended completely to supersede the hierarchy's understanding of a nation's right to restrict immigration on behalf of the common good. "I'm excited about the Sanctuary movement," Father Davis has said, "because I think it is making the churches be what the churches ought to be." That is not the voice of Saint Augustine or Saint Thomas Aquinas speaking. In 1923 the Protestant magazine *Christian Century* described immigrants as "mechanical men who can do all of the work of the world as unthinking, unfeeling automatons." Surely the possibility existed for a revision of that profoundly un-Christian sentiment short of subscribing to the essentially secular platitudes of immigrationism? Yet here is *Christian Century,* sixty years later, endorsing Sanctuary: "The biblical moral order transcends the morality of the civil order, and on those frequent occasions when the two come into conflict, the biblical imperatives have a greater claim on us." Apparently the editors believe they have reached a conclusion, when of course they are only restating the premise. The Vatican strongly advocates, and in fact insists upon, family reunification across oceans and between continents; yet the promise of reunification of families in Heaven is not Catholic doctrine, as long as the doctrine of Hell continues to be preached. Reading *Pacem in Terris,* John XXIII's encyclical addressed to the inadequacy of nation-states and the international system, to which the Pope appears to prefer a world government, one has to ask whether His Holiness had considered in this context the Tower of Babel. It seems strange that Teilhard's concept of the "noosphere" drawing the organic and human worlds together should have been the object of a monition by a Church many of whose officials distrust the concept of national sovereignty, while supporting unlimited migration and the forced melding of international populations.

A sea change seems to have occurred since World War II in the Roman Catholic understanding of the right to immigration, as well as of emigration; partly in response to the international migrations of peoples during the past half-century caused by overpopulation of the Third World, and partly to the political instability and economic collapse, repressive governance, nationalistic excess, and racial and ethnic conflict that have marked this period of history. In addition to these external factors, the Church's own councils have influenced its attitude toward migration, in particular Vatican II (1962–65) which stressed ecumenism and international cooperation, thus underscoring the magisterium's long-standing suspicion of the nation-state. As Simcox suggests, related events have led the Church to view mass migration less as a social phenomenon to be addressed by national governments than as part of the working out of a divine plan for the universalization of human history and thus, in effect, for its sacralization. Pius XII was the first Pope to recognize an explicit though conditional right to migrate: "Public authorities unjustly deny the rights of persons if they block or impede emigration or immigration except where grave requirements of the common good, considered objectively, demand it." John XXIII believed that the state has a grave moral obligation to accept immigrants, asserting, "The fact that one is a citizen of a particular State should not prevent anybody from being a member of the human family as a whole, nor from having citizenship in the world community"; Pope Paul VI in 1967 affirmed the right of "every human being" to leave his native country for whatever reason in search of better living conditions, and to return to it at will. Two years later the Bishops convened for a Vatican conference that updated and codified the teaching of the Church in respect of the rights of immigrants. No Pope, however, has been as uncompromising as John Paul II regarding the obligation of nations—in particular of wealthy nations—to receive immigrants. (A passage in his recent book, *Crossing the Threshold of Hope,* in which he praises his native Poland as a state compounded of many nationalities and religions and marked by qualities of tolerance and openness, perhaps offers a clue to the Holy Father's attitude.) "Migration related to underdevelopment is a challenge which we must face with courage and determination," he wrote in *L'Osservatore Romano,* "since it involves the defense of the human person"—a clear indication of the perceived philosophical and moral connection between immigration and other volatile issues relating to human dignity, including contraception and abortion. Indeed, the Pope's most enthusiastic remarks on the subject—as in his message for World Migration Day 1992, which hailed the countries of the Americas as the creations of immigrants—are an extension of the "nation of immigrants" argument to an entire hemisphere; while his assertion that "When a nation has the courage to open itself to immigration, it is rewarded with increased prosperity, a solid social renewal and a vigorous impetus toward new economic and human goals" might have been ghosted for him by Julian Simon.

"When a stranger sojourns with you in your land, you shall not do him wrong. The stranger who sojourns with you shall be to you as the native among you, and you shall love him as yourself; for you were strangers in the land of Egypt: I am the Lord your God" (Lev. 19:33–34). This Old Testament passage has been frequently adverted to by immigration enthusiasts wishing to prove that the acceptance and generous reception of immigrants is a divine commandment. The word for "stranger" —"sojourner"—employed in the Hebrew text is *ger,* meaning what we today call a resident alien: a type that was common in Palestine after the conquest. As Matthew Welde has noted, what is crucial in this and similar Old Testament verses is that the *ger* had made himself known to the Israeli authorities, who in turn had agreed to allow him to abide among their people. *Tshabi* meant the stranger or sojourner whose residency had not been accepted as permanent, whose children were liable to slavery, and who was himself barred from the redistributionary benefits of the Jubilee years; in the time of Christ, Jews refused to break bread with Gentiles and foreigners. Shortly after World War II, a Catholic Bishop appearing before Congress testified to the existence of an ancient right, "the right of asylum for innocent persons that protects those who flee over borders to escape injustice, persecution, or terror." The United States, the Bishop declared, had been built upon the basis of this right, which he claimed to originate in the Christian Middle Ages as the right of a persecuted man to flee inside a church and cry sanctuary.[33] In fact, nearly all cases involving sanctuary referred to in the Old Testament and recorded in classical and medieval times rested not on Holy Writ but on legal code and custom; moreover, this right of sanctuary normally was observed for a limited period of time only, and granted to malefactors guilty of a type of misbehavior we recognize today as civil disobedience. It is certainly a mistake, as Samuel Francis has explained, to assume that a tradition of sanctuary, originating in the Judeo-Christian conscience and inspired by the Holy Spirit, has been shaped and sharpened by the intervening institutions of Western civilization and delivered to us as a hallowed norm. Rather, it was abandoned when it began to obstruct the uniform law that replaced the arbitrary and localized practices with which it was meant to contend. Finally, the very idea of a social contract is contravened by the extension of our contractual obligations to all men. While indiscriminate generosity may be itself a sort of immigration policy, indiscriminate benevolence is not an ethic. Also, it is imprudent: "Receive a stranger into your home and he will upset you with commotion, and will estrange you from your family" (Sir. 11:24).

For Julian Simon, who believes that receiving ever more immigrants allows us to do good for others while doing well for ourselves, immigration poses no ethical dilemma. Hence, "We do *not* need to consider the ethical basis of simply drawing a boundary line around our nation [hasn't that already been done?] and saying that those who are lucky enough to be born within the line are entitled to wealth and opportunity that we choose to deny to others for selfish reasons." Surely, Simon is enviable for his almost unique ability to read the world like an open book, lacking which lesser minds have felt constrained to spend somewhat more time and thought on the questions he so casually dismisses.

Someone has said admiringly of Renny Golden, a former nun and a founder of the Religious Task Force on Central America, that she "cannot be content with helping the person she sees in front of her because she thinks globally, in sociopolitical context. 'They [the illegal immigrants] come representing a people,' she says. 'They don't say, "Save me and my family!" They say, very clearly, "In the name of God help us." They mean us—El Pueblo—not simply me.'" Clergy and officials of the various American churches have worked at convincing their laities, and the American public at large, that the Christian response to the phenomenon of international migration means subordinating personal loyalties to transnational ones, and self-imposed cultural and political blindness. (Transnationalism is never the ideal of Third World clerics, as instanced by the reaction of a San Salvador Bishop to the passage of Proposition 187 in 1994: "a racist and xenophobic measure has poisoned relations among the inhabitants of Los Angeles.") The most forthright opposition to this holistic, pseudo-religious ethic comes from the proponents of situation ethics, most notably Garrett Hardin. While Hardin's game-management approach to the problems of humanity and his lifeboat ethic (hit them with an oar) are unreconcilable with the Judeo-Christian

tradition, they are entirely consonant with the utilitarian ratio-
nalism that increasingly provides the moral basis for American
society—though not when decisions regarding immigration
are being considered.

"I think there are many instances in which dealing quanti-
ties into the game ... permits us to reinterpret traditional
ethics in a manner suitable to practical men faced with practical problems." Hardin urges that one contemplate three pre-
cepts before practicing philanthropy on an international or
global scale: (1) Motives don't matter. (2) You cannot do only
one thing at once. (In other words, the law of unintended consequences *always* applies.) (3) *"And then what?...."* Christians
must of course object that motives *do* matter, and that situation
ethics fail to envision the possibility of an action of God's grace,
including the intervention of the Divine Mercy, to supplement
feeble and ineffectual human action. Hardin's belief that
"Ethics must become numerate, quantitative," ignores Aristotle's warning that scientific arguments cannot be applied to
moral ones. Nevertheless, when Hardin asks whether "In all
realism, must I be 'my brother's keeper' when there are hundreds of millions of brothers out there crying to be cared for?"
his concern is both realistic and prudential, and to that extent at
least acceptable in the light of Christian teaching.

Hardin denies that we must do whatever we can simply for
the sake of doing it; Aquinas affirmed that we must do what is
justly required of us. If Hardin's ethic is depersonalized, so, in
a different sense, is that of, say, the U.S. Council of Bishops,
supposedly grounded in Thomistic thought. By contrast, Saint
Thomas's ethical sensibility is truly personal, because truly
Christian. Aquinas writing on charity in the *Summa Theologica*
is light-years removed from the modern Catholic Left when he
argues that real charity is (1) natural, (2) divine, and (3) directed
at those closest to God. According to Thomistic philosophy, our
obligations are to those connected to us by nature, to friends
rather than to strangers, and to one's country rather than to the
world. Contrary to the fallacies of Rousseau, but consonant with
the understanding of Burke ("to be attached to the subdivision,

to love the little platoon we belong to in society, is the first principle . . . of public affections") and of Niebuhr, our place in the hierarchy of persons in our society determines to whom we bear responsibility. Considered in this context, Hardin's anti-traditional morality reveals a traditional aspect: "Universalism is unattainable and individualism is not enough. . . . there will always be an important role for the altruism that is one step below universalism. That is the attitude we call 'patriotism.'" Universalists tend to believe that love of one's own is selfish, though in truth it is the only *real* love—and true love is never selfish. The most selfish act imaginable would be to pull down the gates and let them all come in, thereby assuring that our children and grandchildren—and our friends, neighbors, and compatriots, and *their* children and grandchildren—will be subjected to the equal distribution at home of the poverty and misery that were formerly the world's.

"As Christians," the Presbyterian Church announced in a recent statement, "we recognize that the boundaries of God's kingdom are not the same as the boundaries of nations. Citizenship in this kingdom, which comes through faith in Jesus Christ, is based on a radically different standard than the nations of the world. In God's kingdom, national borders have no ultimacy." As the statement suggests, the immigration crisis is a serious temptation to the churches to confuse the worldly with the otherworldly, what is owing to Caesar with what is owing to God. Undoubtedly, the fact that immigrationism has become a false religion—indeed, an idol—goes far to account for this confusion. Whereas the mission of the churches is to teach Truth and to foster and extend the spirit of charity, the job of the state is to maintain the degree of temporal order that the churches—and other institutions—require to fulfill that mission. In spite of a belief, widespread since the eighteenth century, that the Christian religion is a conservative force in the world, and secular government a progressive or revolutionary one, the opposite is actually the case. ("I have come to light a fire upon the earth, and how I wish that it were already burning.") The churches, which regularly accuse the state of encroaching on their role and their responsibilities, are inconsistent in their implicit demand that the state act more like the churches by assuming the universal responsibilities with which they—and only they—have been entrusted. Niebuhr, warning that Christianity must not be historicized, admitted that the "immoralism" of society results from the particularism of groups, which he nevertheless believed to be a source of virtue as well as of "demonic fervor." If only because Christianity is the religion of self-sacrifice, a nation of Christians ought to treat circumspectly the notion of a Christian nation. A man may be morally justified in laying down his life for his friend; but a government that sacrifices the lives of its citizens to the welfare of strangers has no justification, either in law or in religion, for its act.

As the crusade for permanent peace achieved by the establishment of a New World Order in fact assures an era of perpetual warfare, so the opening of their borders by the nations of the West in the interest of alleviating Third World chaos would only guarantee the spread of chaos globally. "I do not believe," Flannery O'Connor wrote, "that Christ abandoned us to chaos." The Western nations, degenerate as they have become, continue to represent systems of relative order in a world that succumbs a little more each day to radical disorder. Can the salvation of man arise from chaos?

—

THE IMMIGRATION PROBLEM BY DEFINITION IS A MIGRATION problem as well, produced by human dislocations, beginning around 1945, on a massive scale such as humanity has not witnessed in thousands of years. Paul Craig Roberts predicts a catastrophic future, described by the French novelist Jean Raspail as "a world of two 'camps,' North and South, separate and unequal, in which the rich will have to fight and the poor will have to die if mass migration is not to overwhelm us all." Immigration, emigration, migration: These Three Horsemen of the Apocalypse threaten an international crisis of universal proportions, of which America's national crisis is a subset, though encompassing every moral and historical contradiction. Raspail understands the situation as being fundamentally the war of the Good against the Bad, in which virtue and evil exist principally in the minds of the contenders. For this reason, he concludes, no satisfactory resolution to the crisis can be found within the parameters of our existing moral system, since to accept all those who wish to come to the West would destroy us, while to refuse them would be tantamount to condemning them to destruction. Without question, migration poses a grave moral conundrum to those concerned—which is the five billion plus human beings alive in the world today. For this reason, it is vitally important that the problem should not be presented moralistically, stated in terms of slogans and clichés, trivialized by posturing and self-serving sentimentalities, and denied the scrupulous moral and philosophical consideration it demands. "Democratic civilization is the first in history to blame itself because another power is working to destroy it," says Jean-François Revel. As a response to current international developments, this is an utterly irresponsible and inadequate reaction: comical and terrible at the same time. If that is the best face the West can put upon its looming destruction, then probably it deserves its fate.

Fairchild recognized "four great types" of migration—immigration, invasion, conquest, and colonization—whose causes are variously economic, political, social, and religious. Of these, the first is the earliest and by far the most significant, though all four causes tend to combine in complex ways. He defined *invasion* as the penetration of a higher civilization by a virile people who invigorate its stock without influencing its culture, and *conquest* as "almost the reverse of an invasion." Here the representatives of the higher culture are the aggressors in "an overflow of civilization, of manners, of organization, of government—not to any great extent of population," imposing upon the lesser society its own political system but refraining from wanton taking of human life and property. According to his conception, *colonization* is typically the action of an overpopulated state seeking commercial rather than military or political aggrandizement, and a better future for its citizens. Finally, Fairchild understood *immigration* as the passage of families or individuals on their own initiative from one developed country to another, usually a new and thinly populated one, in which they expect to remain permanently. Immigration, he emphasized, is a modern development, "a phenomenon of peace" in which only greatly civilized people take part. *All* receiving countries, Fairchild insisted, are more democratic, individualistic, and latitudinarian than sending ones, and also more strenuous in terms of the demands imposed by human existence there. And lastly, "Both of the two states concerned in an immigration movement are well established, and on approximately the same stage of civilization. Immigration can take place only over what Professor [William] Sumner calls a single culture-area." Since major sending countries such as Mexico, El Salvador, and Nicaragua; Ghana and Nigeria; Haiti, Vietnam,

China, and South Korea are plainly neither on the same plane of civilization as the United States nor within the same "culture-area," what the United States experiences today is, according to Fairchild's scheme, far more on the order of invasion than of immigration.

A poll taken early in the 1970s by the Kettering Foundation indicated that a full third of the total population of Latin America (estimated to reach 595 million by the year 2000) wished to emigrate, and that 90 percent of that third hoped to go to the United States. John Tanton has correctly observed that the world population has already grown beyond the solution offered by international migration. "If developed nations took in all the growth of the less-developed nations, they would have to accommodate 66 million persons yearly. Then the developed nations would have an annual growth rate of 5.6 percent and a doubling time of 12.5 years, clearly an impossible solution." Here again is evidence of a truth that the churches, international business interests, advocates of the right of international movement, and academic theorists of a classical liberal or libertarian bent prefer to ignore: "Numbers matter." Maurice Cranston called freedom of movement "the first and most fundamental of man's liberties," while Alan Dowty, in his recent and much-noted book *Closed Borders,* insists that the increasing economic interdependence of nations makes this freedom more important today than it ever was, and that those governments which attempt to restrict it will soon find themselves fighting a losing battle. "Because it is a last line of defense in the realization of other rights, the right of personal self-determination could well be considered the capstone of human rights." Dowty says that classical free-market economists believed nation-states should be indifferent so far as their territories and the boundaries enclosing them are concerned, and that free trade implies immigration and emigration as necessary corollaries: The invisible hand will correct disparities between population and resources, and ease political and social tensions. As examples or models of an "open world," he cites the Mediterranean region in ancient times, the British Commonwealth until recent years—in particular, the era preceding the Great War—and the United States until the 1920s. While Dowty seems not to comprehend that the factors leading governments today to restrict freedom of movement are the same ones that make that freedom an impossible ideal in the contemporary world, he does recognize the impracticability of unrestricted entry in a world encompassing enormously disparate cultural systems, economic levels, and political differences, and marked by vastly disproportionate population aggregates. Other advocates of freedom of movement, sharing Dowty's concern with the rising tide of restrictionism, have suggested that a way to preserve the ideals of mobility and the transferable nature of civil and human rights is to recognize that these have never been fully realized at any time in history, but rather existed in modified form.[34]

Numerous critics of Western immigration policies have stressed that the receiving countries, sharing the same boat together, need to coordinate their actions in such a way that increased restriction on the part of one nation does not inexorably produce added pressure upon the others. But attempts by governments of the West, and in particular that of the United States, to alleviate international migration and the problems associated with it by indirect methods have been an unqualified failure. A favorite strategy is to combine stricter immigration controls with generous attempts to integrate arrived immigrants within the sodality, while trying to stem further immigration by increasing foreign aid and extending preferential trade policies to the sending countries. So far, it has not achieved the desired effect. Dowty suggests that the United States consider "restructuring" certain of its "occupations" or industries, including agriculture, which has become increasingly mechanized since World War II. He does not say, however, what the impact of this might be upon our native-born farm laborers. Michael S. Teitelbaum, in *Latin Migration North,* deals comprehensively with the impracticability of attempting to stem migration by stimulating and subsidizing economic growth and industrialization in the sending countries. Naturally, proposals to bolster the economies of Mexico and the Caribbean island states by opening American markets to their products provoke strong opposition from domestic producers. Moreover, according to Teitelbaum, "recent economic policies in the United States combined with Latin American borrowing policies in the late 1970s ... have resulted unintentionally in increased pressures favoring international migration, both legal and illegal." National (and racial) pride makes direct economic development aid from the United States politically unpopular in many countries, including Mexico (though pride has not prevented the government in Mexico City from accepting billions of dollars in direct investments). Teitelbaum offers Cuba as an excellent example of the direct, confused, and often contradictory linkage between America's immigration and domestic policies and its foreign policy options. Finally, Murphy's ubiquitous Law always obtains: "no one knows (indeed, no one *can* know) which U.S. policy mix toward [say] Central America will most effectively constrain outward immigration flows."[35]

Though immigrationists have always disliked to admit it, benevolent acts even have unintended consequences—most of them unwanted as well. Proponents of generous immigration policies at home are very often the same people who lie awake at night fretting about rising population levels throughout the Third World. Fairchild, having considered the effect of immigration on sending countries, concluded seventy years ago that emigration did little to lessen population increase in the crowded European nations—a finding that has been confirmed by recent scholarship in several fields. Virginia Abernethy (author of *Population Politics: The Choices That Shape Our Future*) believes that the prospect *alone* of immigration has pronatalist effects on sending nations, since the opportunity to emigrate causes local population limits to be disregarded. Garrett Hardin cites studies purporting to show that a decrease in population pressure produces an increase in fertility in animal species, and suggesting that human beings too respond rationally to fluctuations in their populations. "We can confidently predict that removing excess fertility from a poor and overpopulated country will produce a rise in fertility." And Kingsley Davis and Leon Bouvier argue that emigration, by acting as a safety valve, permits countries with burgeoning populations to postpone controlling these in a manner that would make emigration unnecessary, and is therefore conducive to greater population increase.

A similar correlation appears to exist between economic development in the sending countries and the number of emigrants they produce, since those nations which have made the greatest economic progress in the last quarter of a century have also exported the most people. For example, Mexico, which during the better part of the postwar era enjoyed one of the fastest-growing economies in the world, was generating a swelling migration, internal as well as external, even before the economic crisis that developed in the early 1980s. Douglas S. Massey has attempted to explain the phenomenon by suggesting that low wages and retarded economic development are less a spur to migration than are the uncertainties caused by the introduction of capital-intensive development to Third World countries, whose exploding populations discover the web of modern transport and communication increasingly available to them; while Sir James Goldsmith hazards that emigration in search of work destroys family structure and aggravates the social chaos to which nations of the Third World are increasingly subject. Whatever the reasons, the burden of accumulated evidence shows that mass immigration to the United States helps the relative few who emigrate, and plunges the billions of people who remain at home into deeper misery. By *"la fuga de cerebros"* Mexico each year loses thousands of wealthy professionals and businessmen, skilled craftsmen, and young college graduates to the United States. In 1993, the United Nations Population Fund identified some of the harmful effects migration has on the emigrants' home countries, and even on the emigrants themselves. Claimed economic benefits to poor countries from generous immigration policies on the part of rich ones, an agency report said, have yet to be proven: According to "The State of World Population 1993," Africa in recent years lost one-third of its highly educated male population to "brain drain." The report also denied that remittances serve to redress the imbalance between rich and poor nations, to relieve rural poverty, and to alleviate disparities between rural and urban areas in countries of emigration. Julian Simon, in *How Do Immigrants Affect the Economy?*, declines to offer an opinion regarding brain drain, being content to note that it is "unfortunately" extraneous to his argument. But the practice of training foreign students in the United States for skilled work that they have no opportunity to practice—or practice usefully—at home is morally dubious, and so is a policy of accepting immigrants who represent the most hardworking, talented, and energetic from among their people, whose need for them is self-evidently greater than our own. Indeed, some sending countries have demanded financial recompense from receiving ones for migrated workers, while others have claimed that states have an obligation *not* to stimulate mass emigrations of economic refugees.

Louis Adamic suggested in *My America* that "America has been for too long a vent for European discontent. Let the European masses for the time stay where they are, without chance of escape; and let them bring their socio-economic-political-cultural crisis, which is at least a hundred years old, to a head and solve their problems while we work out our own. I believe that by adopting this policy we shall, in the long run, be doing the best we can for the future of Europe and America and all humanity." Today Garrett Hardin argues that restrictionist policies will help in conserving our national strength, which alone allows us to give aid to the rest of the world. Characteristically, Simon rejects this argument, for the reason that immigrants, he says, help to augment that strength rather than to sap it. Yet, as John Tanton points out, the countries that accept the most immigrants are those that export the most food: the United States, Canada, Argentina, Australia, and New Zealand. "What would happen if the populations in these fortunate nations were allowed to grow until their food-exporting capacity were overtaken by domestic food needs? Whose interest would such a turn of events serve? The whole cannot exceed the sum of its parts." By taking the Third World to itself, the United States will *become* the Third World, which is no more than its peoples with their habit and culture of poverty. George Kennan compares the process to that of water seeking its own level, an equalization of overpopulation and poverty within and outside of the United States. Richard Lamm believes America is most serviceable to the world as a model of the sustainable society that has stabilized its population and put a brake on consumption in order to mitigate its impact upon the global environment. As such, he argues, it would be a far more effective "beacon" than it can hope to be by offering a haven to a statistically insignificant proportion of the international population.

Immigration can affect immigrant individuals adversely, as well as migrating populations. For years, FAIR has denounced the exploitation of illegal immigrants by powerful economic interests—a position that Simon condemns as condescending in its presumption that those who adopt it know better than the immigrant himself what is good for him. Some years ago, Richard Estrada of the *Dallas Morning News* effectively disposed of the argument that no matter how degraded the immigrants' condition in America it is still superior to what they experienced in their native land, and anyway, their contribution to the national economy is beneficial, by remarking that it is exactly congruent with the Southern defense of slavery in the antebellum period. As there was no halfway solution to the slavery issue short of abolition, so there is none to the evil of latter-day peonage other than the curtailment of immigration, in particular illegal immigration. But more than exploitation, corruption threatens unsophisticated arrivals to modern-day America. Immigrants to the United States a century ago were introduced into a youthfully energetic, roughly competitive, and ruggedly individualist society, whose policy was to show them no favor beyond admittance and to offer them no more than the little material aid it gave its native-born citizens. By contrast, those coming here today are welcomed by the apparatus of a demoralizing welfare state and a society in moral crisis whose values are hostile to the best that the immigrants bring with them (and which their defenders applaud). Whereas the conditions of American life in the nineteenth century turned at least some of those huddled masses into pioneers, those of the late twentieth century have the potential to change adventurers into petty chiselers, sturdy peasants into welfarites, pious men and women into something worse than pagans, and families into aggregates of atomized individuals. As Joseph Sobran quips, "Give us your tired, your poor, and we will sterilize them." Contrary to the immigrationist's sour view of his opponent, the restrictionist—as Fairchild observed at the beginning of the century—is in some ways the best friend the immigrant ever had.

The enthusiastic view of international migration as an unparalleled historical opportunity is associated with the elite classes of the West and especially those of the United States, for whom it is theoretically appealing as well as institutionally compelling, since a global economy, culture, and technology would benefit an international elite at the expense of the middle and laboring classes of the individual nations. For this reason, members of that elite can afford to affect a disengaged, almost lofty manner when addressing issues related to the international displacement of populations. Raspail's imagination strikes at dead center when he has the president of France imagine the musings of the Grand Mufti of Paris on the subject of inequalities between races and peoples: "just a question of rotation. . . . different ones on top at different times." This philosophical stance is substantially a cover for the conviction of America's ruling class that the American people, being smug, self-righteous, selfish, and racist, *deserve* to lose their country to the nonwhite peoples of the world ("We are being transformed"). "You cannot indict a people," said Burke. The American overclass has been doing exactly that for several generations now, but even if its view of the United States as the world's number one debtor nation, morally as well as financially speaking, is correct, then surely the act appropriate to repentant nations is not self-immolation. It is for God to orchestrate patterns of historical irony, and for men to protect what they have and have made, collectively as individually. Love of the unique civilization that constitutes one's patrimony is itself a conscientious act, and so is the motto that would have us take short views and trust in God for the rest.

THE CULTURAL CRISES IN THE LIVES OF NATIONS ARE INVARIABLY moral crises as well, as Max Oelschlaeger has observed. As the sectional crisis in the antebellum period was the supreme convulsion of the young American Republic, so the cultural warfare at the end of the twentieth century is the preeminent agony of the prematurely sclerotic nation. While abortion, pornography, and school prayer are notable issues in this "culture war," environmentalism and immigration, though less obvious sources of dispute, are fundamentally implicated in the outbreak of hostilities. These closely related subjects are alike in raising practical questions concerning the future of the country and of the ecological matrix that supports it, and moral ones having to do with individual versus communitarian rights, the claims of living generations as opposed to the claims of posterity, and the responsibilities nations have to act as defenders of their societies and stewards of their lands. Although the immigration debate is beginning to move from its long-standing emphasis on individual justice toward a more comprehensive ethical level, so far the welfare of nations has proved something less than a trump card in the hands of the restrictionists. The environmental argument, however, operating on a third and still more inclusive level, could prove to be the ace of spades: theoretically compelling at first and in time, perhaps, politically effective.

Although in its sophisticated modern form the environmentalist case against immigration comes closer than any other to being a new and original contribution to a four-hundred-year-old controversy, even so it is not without historical precedent. As early as 1896 Francis Walker, commissioner general of the

Immigration Service, implicitly linked environmental destruction with the great numbers of immigrants then arriving in the
United States; in 1923 the *Saturday Evening Post* asked why millions of southeastern Europeans should be admitted, since even
in the absence of further immigration the population of the
country was projected to reach the "enormous figure" of 200
million people by the end of the century. (Nor is a frequently
heard, if sublimely irrelevant, type of argument *against* the population factor new: Piatt Andrew, writing in the *North American Review* in 1914, noted that if the entire population of the
United States were settled in Texas, the population density per
square mile would be only two-thirds as great as that of England.) Early in the century, the environmentalist movement
had roughly the same influence that the anti-immigrationist
movement has enjoyed for most of the period since World War
II—which is to say, almost none. It had John Muir, but it still
awaited Aldo Leopold; its ideas were inchoate, unorganized,
and—more significantly—unmobilized. "In a sense," David
North has observed, "the struggle over immigration policy is
like a struggle over environmental policy: the narrow-focused
opponents of immigration enforcement, along with their
diverse allies, like the narrowly-focused opponents of pollution
abatement, have much more at stake than those on the other
side of the issue. . . ." Thus, where immigration as well as environmental legislation is concerned, minority opinion rather
than the will of the majority has tended to prevail.

More broadly focused opponents of restriction continue to
include the major environmentalist organizations, whose
orthodox liberal views have caused them to support a generous
immigration policy, or at least to refrain from criticizing it.
This is the reason why many organizations promoting immigration control are heavily staffed by environmentalists—not a
few of them refugees from the Sierra Club and similar main-
line institutions—who found their restrictionist ideas unwelcome with their former employers. ("[T]he nastiest of political
issues," Governor Jerry Brown's secretary for resources complained.) In the congressional debate on the 1990 immigration
bill only one conservationist group, Population-Environment

Balance, testified to the likely effects of large-scale immigration on America's national resources, an issue that most environmentalist operations have ignored since immigration began to be a hot topic at the end of the 1970s. Representative Tony Beilenson, a liberal Democrat from Beverly Hills, has been attacked for his opposition to immigration in the interest of population control by fellow liberals like Arnold Torres, executive director of the League of United Latin American Citizens, who in the mid-1980s criticized the collection of data pertaining to the effects of population growth on natural resources and environmental conditions for offering ammunition to the supporters of the Simpson-Mazzoli bill. As a result of such treatment in the past, environmentalists tend to be most comfortable when they are criticizing immigration in the name of some impeccably liberal concern, such as the displacement by immigrants of blacks from their jobs and neighborhoods.

Ben Wattenberg thinks environmentalism is about "the nice crisis," a *faux* concern of a civilization that, being affluent and pretty much at peace, can afford a few luxury causes. He is equally dismissive of the population crisis, which he regards as "the catastrophic handmaiden of environmentalists. Sooo many people, causing sooo much despoliation, and sooo much poverty." Wattenberg counters the assertion that America is becoming overcrowded by strangely arguing that more than a third of its counties are losing population; that it is "over" polluted by claiming that pollution is "lower" than it was two decades ago—despite the increase in population produced largely by immigration. Julian Simon agrees that environmental conditions are improving as the population of the United States continues to expand, as are the nation's water and food supplies; he adds, "To cite resource 'limits' in discussions of immigration policy is unsound geology, incorrect history, and rotten economics." "Contrary to popular belief"—a favorite phrase of his—Simon explains, natural resources "over the long-run" have been getting less scarce, as is proved by their lower cost and greater market availability. "The weight of the evidence suggests that though additional people cause more pollution in the short run, in the long run additional people lead to less pollution, strange as that may seem." The environmental effects of immigration are "no special problem," he suggests, since they are similar to those produced by additional citizens; besides which, "the whole matter of the effects of additional people on the environment is very complex, and fraught with argument and confusion." As Simon well knows, having sown much of it.

It is popular these days to mock the "doomsayers" who wrote and talked at length in the 1960s on the subject of the population bomb. Yet their predictions, Leon Bouvier warns, were substantially correct; indeed, they are even now being realized. It is true that, in global terms, the effects of migration upon the natural world have not been determined. Wattenberg has shrewdly noted that immigration does not increase the human population of the earth, it simply "shifts it around." His implication is that it makes no difference, from either a global or a national point of view, where large concentrations of that population are situated. That implication is wrong, however, since people—whether natives or immigrants—in Western countries use a far greater share of natural resources and place a much greater strain on the natural environment than the residents of Third World countries. One of the more curious aspects of the immigration controversy is the refusal by people concerned about global population growth to support an immigration policy that would go far to halt population increase here in the United States, the only place in the world where we are in a position to do anything about it. Immigrationists, it seems, believe that America, alone among the nations of the world, is exempt from the principle of optimal population attainment, and that ever-increasing numbers of people will prove endlessly beneficial to it. In the two centuries between 1790 and 1990 the population of the United States increased at just under 2 percent a year, an historically unprecedented rate over so long a period of time and one which compares with that of the modern developing nations; in the almost half-century from 1950 to 1990 it grew by 100 million persons, to which another 134 million are projected to be added in the next fifty-five years, making the United States the most rapidly growing industrial nation in the world. In the past ten or fifteen years, more than one-half of all population growth has come from immigration, which within several decades will account for the total growth in population of the country. Apologists for mass immigration reply that the United States still has the lowest population density of any Western nation, with the exception of Australia and Canada. Of course, many Americans would like to keep it that way.

"[Demographic] numbers still count," Ben Wattenberg insists, "not for everything, but for plenty." He means that a positive correlation exists between large populations and national power and wealth. More than seventy years ago William Roscoe Thayer qualified that theory when he wrote, in the context of the immigration debate, that only the character of a nation's people, not their numbers, give it strength. When Simon's *The Ultimate Resource* was published in 1981, William G. Tucker, in his review of the book for the *Washington Post,* called it "the most powerful challenge to be mounted against the principles of popular environmentalism in the last 15 years." Simon's thesis—that human beings are problem solvers who can repair or compensate for any environmental damage the race has done or will do, and the more of them therefore the better—was accepted like passed ammunition in entrepreneurial circles boosting the concept of unlimited growth, and as manna from heaven or at the least inspired wisdom by many Christians, who should have known better. Several years later, in *How Do Immigrants Affect Us Economically?*, Simon purported to describe how population increase stimulates productivity and augments production, how larger cities are more economically efficient than smaller ones, the favorable relationship between great populations and the growth of knowledge, and the equally positive one between population density and economic affluence.

Simon's views on the benefits of exponentially increasing population growth, which even some of his admirers seem to find embarrassing, are not accepted by those concerned about the effects mass immigration has had, and will continue to have, upon the environment of North America. The Sierra

Club in 1989 pronounced the United States to be the most over-populated country in the world, when its ecologically destructive way of life is considered. "Immigrants," Garrett Hardin says, "come to America hoping to increase their consumption of environmental resources. They soon succeed." Immigration from the undeveloped countries to the developed ones, scientists argue, greatly increases the consumption of world resources, adds substantially to existing levels of pollution, and, by destroying farmland, weakens the ability of the receiving countries to produce the food that keeps many of the sending ones from mass starvation. Virginia Abernethy goes so far as to predict that sometime between the years 2007 and 2025, when roughly a quarter of 117 nations will be unable to feed so much as one-half of their populations, the United States will have ceased to be a net exporter of foodstuffs. As long as America remains the "compassionate" acceptor of immigrants, the countries of origin will be deprived of incentives to address their problems of overpopulation and pollution, and the United States itself will be distracted from developing a population policy in respect of immigration, which is arguably the single most effective and practicably responsible action available to it. Twenty-some years ago the Commission on Population and the American Future, chartered by Congress in 1970 and charged with the task of creating a federal policy regarding of population, issued a report that President Nixon rejected on account of its endorsement of abortion, contraception, and sex education. The so-called Rockefeller Commission also recommended that the level of legal immigration be frozen at 400,000 a year, and warned that immigration had the potential to produce considerable population growth in coming decades. However, the commission itself was little interested in immigration policy as a whole, and its recommendations regarding the subject failed to survive the oblivion into which its family-planning proposals were deservedly sunk.

The American religious leadership, highly politicized since the 1950s and even more liberal than the clergy, blames the United States and its military and economic interventions for most of the dislocations in the world today, including environmental ones. Although the churches are paying more attention nowadays than formerly to biblical implications regarding man's responsibility for nature, religious environmentalists consider it selfish of Americans to attempt to ensure America's environmental health while human misery and degradation exist elsewhere on the planet; for them, the top priority on a proper environmentalist agendum would be a substantial reduction in Americans' consumption of natural resources, at home and abroad. Still, a poll conducted by the *United Methodist Register* indicated that 59 percent of the American clergy favor stabilizing population growth over accepting more immigrants when the choice between stabilization and immigration arises, while the U.S. Catholic Bishops have acknowledged, in a paper issued in 1991, that "Even though it is possible to feed a growing population, the ecological costs of doing so ought to be taken into account. . . . Our mistreatment of the natural world diminishes our own dignity and sacredness, not only because we are destroying resources that future generations of humans need, but because we are engaging in actions that contradict what it means to be human." Popes Paul VI and John Paul II have recognized the damaging effect of demographic growth on the natural world, and John Paul, in a message issued for the World Day of Peace in 1992, described ecological crisis as a "moral issue." According to Rabbi David Saperstein, director of the Action Center of Reform Judaism in Washington, D.C., "The Jewish community has a many-thousand-year-old religious concern for protecting God's creation, so for us [population control] is a religious obligation." On the other hand, a spokeswoman for the center, in reply to an interviewer's question whether approved means of population stabilization included curtailing immigration, answered, "My general sense is that we feel the United States has a special responsibility for persecuted people and to open its arms." Roy Beck, in a survey he made for the *Social Contract,* was unable to find a single denomination prepared to endorse the preservation of the American environment if preservation meant controlling population growth.

Protestants, Jews, and Roman Catholics, he concluded, bear direct responsibility for the recent rapid increase in human numbers in the United States, owing to their stubborn support of mass immigration.

At the crux of the population issue is the fundamental disagreement between the secular viewpoint, which sees the world as an end in itself, and the religious one, which regards it as a thing that "passeth away," ultimately to be replaced by a new Heaven and a new Earth. "How Western man has pretty well succeeded in locking himself into a suicidal course of action by clinging to a concept of the absolute sanctity of life is a topic that calls for deep inquiry." For Garrett Hardin, the fatal weakness of most contemporary ethical thinking is its assumption that human life is the highest good, or, in to him archaic terms, that it is sacred. But what, he asks, do we mean by human life? The more than five billion individual human beings walking around on the earth today? Or human life as a generalized entity that includes posterity? In Hardin's view, a "time-blind absolute ethical principle like that implied by the shibboleth, 'the sanctity of life,'" and endorsed by "amiable, individualistic, present-oriented, future-blind Western ethicists," produces worse misery than does what he calls the "situationist, ecological alternative," which replaces the idea of the sanctity of existing life with that of the "sanctity of the carrying capacity." Adopting Joseph Fletcher's motto, "We should give if it helps, not if it hurts," Hardin suggests that consequences be made the measure of morality, since if the ends do not justify the means then nothing does, and because all too often the motive of the giver is self-interested and the benefactor himself unconcerned for the unintended consequences of his actions. Plainly, situation ethics according to Christian understanding are a satanic temptation, being as far removed as it is possible to get from the Christian obligation to treat every individual as one would treat oneself, to do no evil in the name of a greater good, and beyond that to trust and have faith in God. It is a moral code for those who believe that the world is indeed its own end, and that any action whose final goal is to maintain that world for as long as it is humanly or naturally possible to do so is therefore a just one. Hardin is wrong to accuse "traditional ethics" of virtually ignoring the good of posterity. But he is correct in claiming that the essence of ecological ethics is their regard for posterity. There is, after all, nothing un-Christian or nontraditional in the idea that responsible stewardship is concerned foremostly with what has been directly entrusted to it, that it manages for the future and has posterity in mind, that it entails unpleasant moral choices, and that its obligation increases with proximity. The religious imperative to "care for creation," in Oelschlaeger's phrase, indicates that the Western churches are on the wrong side of the immigration issue. If so, it is possible that they may in time discover the fact for themselves, as they have already begun to renovate their exaggeratedly anthropocentric understanding of Scripture. (Saint Augustine thought that "Be fruitful and multiply" referred not to the production of human offspring but to gifts, or actions, of the Holy Spirit.)

The environmentalist concept of carrying capacity, defined as "the number of individuals who can be supported without degrading the natural, cultural, and social environment," has found favor with and been adopted (and adapted) by scientists, economists, scholars, and critics as diverse as Garrett Hardin, Virginia Abernethy, Herman Daly, George Kennan, Thomas Fleming, and Edward Abbey, who a year before his death in 1989 put the thing in a nutshell when he remarked, "True human freedom, economic freedom, social freedom, remain basically linked to physical freedom, sufficient space, enough land." Useful as a concept, carrying capacity is equally effective as an argument, not only for the reason that it is true but because it is capable of fairly holding the moral high ground in debate, which it raises above narrow considerations of individual justice and also broader ones regarding the integrity of the nation-state—concerns that it does not exclude, but rather subsumes under one that is broader still. As the nation-state is the least onerous and most efficient system available today for the organization of the peoples of the world, so carrying capacity as it is understood in terms of nations is the best formula yet devised for the maintenance of those fragile and ecologically interdependent systems of social, cultural, and natural components called civilizations. The concept of carrying capacity provides the strongest and most comprehensive argument so far developed against mass immigration to America, and the West.

IT IS POSSIBLE THAT REMARKS MADE AT THE BEGINNING OF this book suggest that the author does not believe the economic argument for—or against—immigration has a moral or conscientious dimension. If so, the time has come to dispel that impression. The idea of economic progress has been widely accepted as an essentially moral proposition for several centuries in the Western world, nowhere more so than in America. Though economics was by no means the entire, or even the most important, influence in the nation's founding, Robert Bellah is correct when he says, "The United States was planned for progress. It was commonplace among the country's eighteenth-century founders that economic life was not simply a natural fact of nature, that political economy was a brand of political ethics and its practice an exercise in public morality." The historians Charles and Mary Beard, in the early 1900s, were among the first to inflate this truth into the false claim that the true American ideal had always been wealth, not liberty; rich men rather than free ones—an ahistorical assumption that chose to ignore the social, cultural, and moral differences between a constitutional republic and an economic and military colossus, and the processes that converted the one into the other. Comparison of the immigration debate of the early national period, when the stipulated concern was for the preservation of American constitutionalism against alien agents of French republicanism, with that of today, when, as Thomas Fleming observes, "most of the conversation is about money," exhibits those differences in a distressingly stark light. One reason for the preeminence of economics in the contemporary discussion of immigration is that the United States has become substantially a materialistic society governed almost exclusively by materialists, for whom the language of economics is their *lingua franca* and the logic of utilitarianism the only recognized form of mental activity. Another, as Fleming suggests, is that the extreme tenderness of public discourse in America (a product of the "diversity" created by past immigrations, not by black slavery) restricts the discussion to abstractions, such as money, "because what some Americans worry about cannot be spoken to the network reporters doing on-the-street interviews for the evening news." But perhaps the most important reason is that modern immigration, as Henry Pratt Fairchild recognized several generations ago, really *is* an economic phenomenon, and the predominant motive of immigrants is the economic incentive, which Fairchild assumed to be inferior to the political and religious motive but which the American public class of today feels confident that the American people will respond to sympathetically.

Of course, economic progress and national wealth are more than a moral idea. Viewed in the context of claims asserted by other interests held by human societies, they are an objective as well as a subjective good which private citizens and government leaders alike have a duty to further. Julian Simon insists that his primary interest in promoting immigration is the welfare of American citizens, while that of the citizens of the sending countries is for him a secondary concern. Yet, almost in the same breath, he says, "It is not clear why immigration is a salient issue now," and elsewhere muses that "Nowadays, in the U.S., it is difficult to determine the motivation for opposition to immigration." In an appendix to *The Economic Consequences of Immigration* he claims to probe beyond economic issues to the political and philosophical dimensions of his subject. In fact, he dodges these and other noneconomic considerations, since "arguments based on 'natural rights' all seem to be inconclusive," and "Though [cultural homogeneity] . . . is largely a matter of taste, one could investigate the consequences of restrictive policies based on [it] for such issues as economic freedom. But as I know of no systematic evidence on the topic, I shall leave it. . . ."

Simon's arguments—which are mainly just unsubstantiated statements that people who want to agree with him have no interest in challenging, or even questioning—have been heard in the United States for more than a hundred years, typically from men of business and from the business press. A contributor to the *North American Review* in 1882, estimating that the "brain and muscle" of each immigrant was worth $51,000 in capital, calculated that the United States "made" $57.2 million in 1881 from immigration. Frederick Knapp, a New York State commissioner of immigration, figured every immigrant to have an economic value of $1,125; while another *Review* contributor, in 1908, claimed that the United States enjoyed a 4:1 credit ratio with regard to its importation of aliens. In 1892 the *New York Journal of Commerce* complained that "There can be nothing more injurious to the prosperity of the American people than this senseless clamor against free immigration. . . . [Immigrants] are a real addition to the wealth of the country." The *Wall Street Journal* in 1906 guessed that a million uneducated but healthy immigrants would increase the national wealth by $100 million per annum; a couple of years later a New York congressman asserted that the United States had always required the immigrant in order to amass wealth, and probably always would. An article in the *Saturday Evening Post* deplored the effect the Great War was having in cutting off immigration, since "We cannot expand industrially without a continually expanding supply of labor." The economist Bernhard Ostrolenk, writing in the *North American Review* in 1935, denied that the number of jobs is fixed by "some occult power," and that the period of greatest immigration to the United States—1800 to 1910—had had the effect of decreasing, rather than increasing, employment.

This vulgar economic reductionism—as in calculations that x number of immigrants equals y amount of money—is the sort of comic Babbittry that educated Americans since the 1920s have been taught to deplore. Yet Simon's work, in spite of being a throwback to a vanished era ("Imagine a billion Orientals and Africans and South Americans without education or skills suddenly arriving in the U.S. tomorrow. Everything would at first

be in terrible shape"), has been strangely popular and astound-
ingly influential. For Simon, the notion that immigrants—
immigrants from everywhere, of every kind, in any numbers—
are an unmitigated economic boon to the United States is an
idée fixe. "Though hard to nail down, the beneficial impact of
immigrants upon productivity, additional workers and consumers, is likely to dwarf all other effects of immigrants after
they have been in the country for a few years." For Simon—a
scientist, albeit of a sort—nearly everything is hard to nail
down, accepted not even so much as a matter of faith as of simple assertion, usually qualified by "likelies" and "probablies."
Simon claims that immigrants are better educated on average
than natives and arrive in the country with higher and better-
developed skills, as well as with a wider variety of occupational
backgrounds; that the average immigrant surpasses the average
native American worker in earnings after a few years in the
United States; that the immigrants' characteristic youth and sex
(male) are "a major economic advantage to the receiving native
population" (he doesn't mention that they also point to impend-
ing demographic catastrophe); and that immigrants contribute
more in taxes to the economy than they take from it in benefits.
("Despite the fact that illegal Mexican immigrants use almost
no public services . . . they do pay taxes"; no evidence offered in
support of this statement.) As for the displacement question,
which Simon calls probably the most emotionally charged issue
in the immigration controversy, he denied, in a book published
in 1989, that any of the several then-recent "empirical" studies
of displacement "using a variety of approaches" had found evidence of "across-the-board unemployment caused by immigrants, either in the U.S. as a whole or in particular areas of relatively high immigration," and including among vulnerable
groups such as blacks and women. From these studies, Simon
concluded that the forces for job creation must be at least as
powerful as those for displacement; while conceding that
immigrants employed in a given occupation necessarily have
some adverse effect upon wages and employment among
natives in the same occupation, he also determined that that
effect was more than compensated for by benefits to the general

public gained from lower prices of goods produced by the affected industry.

Numerous scholars and researchers have criticized Simon's work for its dependence on outworn statistics and dated studies, as well as for its sleight-of-hand techniques—such as the conflation of illegal with legal immigrants, which creates the false impression that the two groups are equal in education, skills, and earning power, and which Simon uses to justify his assertion that immigrants exceed natives in terms of economic success within a few years of their arrival. Barry Chiswick, an economist at the University of Illinois, Chicago Circle, has consistently concluded from much the same evidence available to Simon that, economically speaking, the children and later descendants of Mexican immigrants have been relatively unsuccessful. In addition, economists Donald L. Huddle, Arthur F. Corwin, and Gordon J. MacDonald as long ago as 1985 published a devastating critique of the so-called windfall myth of the economic benefits of immigration to the American economy; according to Huddle et al., 30 percent of "Spanish-origin groups" were below the poverty line in 1982, compared with roughly 22.5 percent a decade earlier. From field research among undocumented Mexican families in southern California and Haitian and Dominican ones in New York City, Roger Connor of FAIR found that the longer illegal aliens remain in the United States the more adept they become at availing themselves of social services, including Medicaid and unemployment compensation; while the United States Immigration Service estimated in 1983 that federal, state, and local governments incurred a net loss of $1.26 billion annually for every one million illegals. Over the past twenty to thirty years the type of illegal immigrant, and hence the character of illegal immigration, has changed significantly, a fact that Simon has chosen to ignore in spite of his having read George Borjas's 1985 study documenting the change, which he dismissed by remarking that it will be years before Borjas's conclusions can be either proved or disproved. But Borjas's *Friends or Strangers: The Impact of Immigrants on the U.S. Economy* (1990) contradicts Simon's work by showing that recent immigrants are far more likely than their predecessors to lack skills and employment and to be reliant on the public welfare system, and that the costs of immigration over the past fifteen to twenty years have been enormous. Reviewing Borjas's book in tandem with Simon's *The Economic Consequences of Immigration,* Professor Huddle called Simon's ideas "both oversimplified and extreme"; he added, "Those aspects of Simonism that are not contradicted by Simon himself are contradicted, for the most part, by Borjas later on." David North of the New TransCentury Foundation brushes aside the question of whether illegals pay more in taxes than they receive in transfer benefits by noting that the answer is immaterial, since "If one works in a country, he assumes the obligation of paying taxes to it. . . . [H]ow the balance comes out shouldn't be the deciding point. Because there should not be a drain on the social service system by individuals whom the society and government have decided are not eligible to partic-ipate in the social service system." Nor, he adds, ought the American people—assuming that illegals *do* help to underwrite national benefit programs—to allow themselves to be subsi-dized by a population of poverty-stricken aliens whose pres-ence among them is the result of their deliberate violation of the law of the land.

In 1890 a reviewer of a book by R. Mayo Smith agreed that "constant immigration to a certain extent tends to displace American labor, thus to lower wages and standards of living." More than thirty years later the *New York World* complained that the opponents of an immigration bill being considered by Congress were willing to deny protection for the American working class against the dumping of foreign labor in the United States, similar to that accorded commercial and indus-trial interests by a concurrent bill to prevent American markets from being flooded by foreign goods. Ray Marshall, secretary of labor in the Carter administration, estimated that the unem-ployment rate in the United States in 1979 would have been 3.7 instead of 5.8 percent had illegal aliens not taken two million jobs from American citizens; in 1985, Huddle, Corwin, and MacDonald figured the costs of the displacement of native workers by illegal ones at more than $30 billion in 1982-83.

Assuming the number of illegal workers in the same year to have been 5.5 million, they calculated that illegals accounted for 4.5 percent of the labor force, and that for every 100 of these employed as secondary labor in factories, in outdoor work, and in the service industries, 65 American workers were displaced or kept out of the job market. Moreover, they found evidence that undocumented aliens—who for decades had dominated the agricultural labor force on the Southwest border—had moved inland, where, in a time of rising unemployment, they were rapidly displacing interstate migrant farm workers, mostly blacks and Chicanos. Previously, employers facing shortages of common and unskilled labor had looked to native minority groups to supply them with needed workers; now they had available to them all the cheap unskilled labor they could use—illegal immigrants whom they need not pay the minimum wage or provide with benefits. Huddle, Corwin, and MacDonald outlined the process of displacement: (1) American workers are fired, and replaced by illegal ones; (2) the fired Americans remain unemployed, as they are not informed of job openings that employers prefer to fill with underpaid and docile undocumented aliens; (3) native job seekers at entry level, especially teenagers, cannot find work, which has been taken by illegals; (4) the displaced native workers migrate within the United States in search of jobs already garnered by illegal workers, and of improved labor standards. "Subsidized by the welfare state, many inner-city inhabitants are unwilling to compete with the newcomers. Put another way, job displacement and social assistance entitlements go hand-in-hand to institutionalize what economists call 'structural unemployment' among U.S. minorities, particularly blacks, Puerto Ricans and U.S.-born Chicanos." As Governor Lamm has said, either we can continue to import more unskilled labor or we can train and employ our own poor, but we cannot do both, and we will have to decide.

The justice of a society's deliberately displacing—or allowing to be displaced—its own citizens from their jobs so as to replace them with a servile caste at serfs' wages is so plainly questionable that those willing to promote, or anyway defend, the practice have felt compelled to justify their position by moralistic references to the decline of the work ethic in America. "[F]or whatever reasons," Julian Simon claims, "immigrants are more vigorous than natives," "more competent than available natives at the same wage." The claim that immigrants work harder for less pay than native Americans will was made as early as the 1840s, before America became a nation of spoiled consumers and when it was still a country of hardy and "vigorous" pioneers—which of itself suggests that the argument even in those times was an exercise in dishonesty. In fact, according to Huddle, Corwin, and MacDonald, illegal aliens engaged in common labor quit their jobs with approximately the same frequency as American workers and for the same reasons (that is, those for which laborers usually quit their work), to be replaced by other aliens as cheap and docile as themselves. The truth is, citizen workers find it impossible to compete with illegal ones when the competition between them will be decided by which of them are willing to work the longer hours under the more unpleasant conditions for less pay. Simon and other immigrationists are eager to take unscrupulous and hypocritical employers at their word when they complain that "Americans don't want to work at menial jobs." Vernon Briggs, though admitting that the claim remains a very difficult one for economists either to disprove or substantiate, insists that there is no evidence at all to support it. A former undersecretary of labor, Malcolm Lovell, has noted that as of 1981 nearly 30 percent of the American labor force held the same sort of low-skilled jobs that illegal aliens typically take; while a study made by Ohio University in 1980 for the Labor Department indicated that a majority of teenagers and young people were willing to accept ill-paying jobs in such industries as the fast-food business— contrary to an official for the International House of Pancakes, whom Simon quotes as saying that high school students don't want dishwashing jobs anymore, they want to be president of the company. To the extent that the attitude of the House of Pancakes man represents the thinking of American employers, it probably suggests the estrangement of many middle-class people from lower-class workers, as well as a prejudice against native black employees in favor of Mexican ones. Speculation aside, the fact remains that in every occupational sector in America the majority of those employed are American citizens, indicating that the real question is not whether Americans are ready to perform menial and often unpleasant tasks but whether those other Americans who hire them to do so are willing to pay them fair wage for their services.

American workers *do* refuse to compete with immigrants for jobs that immigrants have created for immigrants, and for jobs that have been "Mexicanized," as Francis Walker observed back in the 1890s. Simon argues that the earnings record with which he credits recently arrived immigrants is the more impressive given the disadvantages they suffer. He does not mention that they are frequently employed in what Huddle calls "the depths of ethnic subcultures," working for extremely cloistered immigrant businesses in which most jobs are filled by members of extended families and their friends: underground cash economies operated off the books. "Apparently Simon has never done an in-depth field study of an exploitative Hispanicized labor market. And, therefore, he has paid little attention to the subcultural behavior of different immigrant groups and what each brings in the way of skills, education, social values and family dependents. Nor does he touch on the furtive, sleazy underground economy of poverty-stricken illegal aliens, the alien-smuggling industry and job-slot and paper-vending business. Here, too, immigrants 'make jobs.'"

George Kennan fears that the inability of a society to fill its labor requirements from its own demographic resources is a serious and perhaps even a fatal weakness, reminiscent of the Roman Empire's reliance on the barbarian hordes to fill its military ranks. In America today, people talk unashamedly of the benefits of cheap labor, encouraged by the enthusiasm of the business and professional classes for the readily exploited workers that transnational migration delivers to them from around the world. Many so-called conservatives, and a substantial portion of the American "conservative" movement, advocate open borders, freedom of international movement, and virtually unlimited immigration to the United States on the ground that it benefits "free" enterprise. They are well rewarded for their services. The Heritage Foundation, a "conservative" think tank that promotes the ideas of Julian Simon and made common cause with Hispanic activists to oppose the employer sanctions provisions of the Immigration Reform and Control Act of 1986, has been significantly underwritten by governments and businesses in the Far East. In the 1960s, "conservatives" assured indignant liberals protesting the impact illegal immigrants were making on native job seekers that the unlawful aliens contributed more to the economy than they took from it. Huddle, Corwin, and MacDonald have explained how American employers benefit from illegals, and how they pass along their profits to the social service sector as costs, unreimbursed. When one considers the seemingly inexhaustible pool of surplus labor in the United States (as evidenced by the national welfare rolls), current assertions that America is on the verge of a labor shortage should be suspect. For Garrett Hardin, they are a "warning signal that someone is seeking a labor subsidy from outside the national system."

If "labor shortage" implies anything, it is the necessity for an increase in wages for young unskilled American workers. "Conservative" economists have argued, however, that Americans are too highly paid; a situation that immigration is certainly likely to remedy. So is the transfer of capital and technology to countries of the Third World, with their hundreds of millions of surplus workers—a process that Neal Soss, chief economist of the First Boston Corporation, predicted will result in "labor supply shock." According to Soss, that transfer would weaken the value and bargaining power of labor in First World countries, striking inflation a major blow and the Western middle classes an even greater one, while enhancing enormously the wealth and power of the international elites. Edward Luttwack has remarked that American supporters of the free trade agreement between the United States and Mexico appear to believe that the loss of some jobs southward across the border will alleviate or put an end altogether to emigration northward. He himself thinks it will have no such effect, since the number of the Mexican unemployed, added to the more than two million additions to the work force annually, is so great that the wholesale transfer to Mexico of *all* America's manufacturing jobs would scarcely reduce the flood of illegal immigrants to the United States. Since the relaxation of national borders in the name of "free trade" has already led to huge numbers of people arriving unexpectedly in the United States and other wealthy countries, opponents of immigration are justified in questioning whether restrictions on the movement of human beings can survive the erosion of those placed on the international transfer of goods and services, given especially the commitment of the global elite to the abolition of both sets of restraints.

"I have heard a great deal about their cheap labor [that is, Chinese immigrants in California and elsewhere on the West Coast]. I do not myself believe in cheap labor. I do not believe cheap labor should be an object of legislation, and it will not be in a republic. You cannot have the wealthy classes in a republic where suffrage is universal, legislate for cheap labor. . . . Labor should not be cheap and it should not be dear; it should have its share and it will have its share." So spoke Senator James G. Blaine on the Senate floor, 14 February 1879. Blaine's argument, that a larger national interest takes precedence over employers' "needs" for slave labor, child labor, and sweat labor, is being heard again in the United States today. As apologists for the peculiar institution attacked the "wage-slavery" of the North and insisted upon the economic necessity for slavery in the South, so defenders of child labor predicted economic ruin if child-labor legislation were enacted to cover mining operations, sugar beet farms, and the Southern mills. But though American industrialists and agriculturalists have always believed large supplies of cheap labor essential to profitability, industry and agriculture accommodated themselves to the loss of slavery and the child-labor system, and eventually profited by it.[36] If, moreover, cheap common labor is good for business, cheap management should be even better. Indeed, the more cynical commentators on the immigration controversy have perceived a certain class bias to be inherent there. Were business executives, lawyers, professors, print journalists, and television anchormen heavily represented among immigrants—legal and illegal—would their native colleagues welcome them as fervently to the United States as they now do drywallers, avacado pickers, cab drivers, and nannies? When, in the 1930s, a variety of refugee stage performers, in addition to thousands of scholars and academicians, arrived from Europe, concerned actors and musicians testifying before a committee of the U.S. House of Representatives demanded legislation that would prevent foreign artists from performing in the United States, and warnings were heard of the imminent takeover of America's institutions of higher learning by foreigners.

Statistical addendum. The number of lawyers in the United States specializing in immigration law rose from three hundred in the 1970s to thirty-six hundred in 1992, according to the rolls of the American Immigration Lawyers Association.

Fairchild concluded that the economic argument has always been "by far the greatest and most universal argument for immigration. . . ." American industry requires immigration; cessation would cripple the nation's basic industries. Thinking it "inconceivable" that the United States should ever have been dependent for any of its great projects on a foreign labor supply, foreign vigor, and a foreign vision, Fairchild himself did not subscribe to this position. John Lukacs, believing mass immigration to have been crucial to America's industrial development and to the necessary expansion of its population, disagrees with Fairchild on the historical importance of immigration to the United States, but emphasizes its destructive effects since the Second World War.

Ironically, the "new immigration" of the 1970s, '80s, and '90s, though defended and praised primarily for economic reasons, is the result of legislation of the 1950s and '60s in which economic considerations had no part. In those far-off days, the American economy appeared impregnable, and the era of migration was barely begun; it occurred to no one to tie immigration ceilings to domestic fertility levels, and to the unemployment rate. Instead, the new law radically redirected American immigration policy away from the national self-interest toward international benevolence, moralistic posturing, and alternative forms of foreign aid. Washington maintained direction with this policy through the 1970s and '80s, as the United States lost its economic dominance and the nations of the Third World slipped into deepening crisis. The Immigration and Nationality Act of 1965 was indeed a historical aberration, supplanting America's historical commitment to its economic development with a devotion to family reunification and the admission of refugees, foreign policy considerations, and a vague shibboleth, "civil rights." It also came to be what Vernon Briggs termed a wild card among the nation's labor-market policies, from which it remained detached.

Linda Chavez thinks that immigrants working for low wages have "saved" certain American industries from destruction. Her claim has been disputed by Michael Teitelbaum, who points out that the problems of the garment industry, for one, have nothing to do with labor factors, but everything to do with structure, undercapitalization, and competition from more efficient foreign competitors. While Simon and Wattenberg gush over the windfall jobs that immigrants create, economists have noted that the United States really needs greater capital and more and better technology, which immigration does not supply. While no one blames the immigrants for America's economic problems, nevertheless the arrival *en masse* of unskilled immigrants self-evidently thwarts the nation's attempts at overcoming problems in productivity, and provides a disincentive to advance toward higher technological levels. "It is . . . difficult," Simon says, "to establish how many jobs would stand open if immigrants do not come, because after a while employers make other arrangements, either by using machines instead of human labor or by reducing the scale of the enterprise." This is nothing short of an admission by Simon that indeed immigration does retard modernization and technological sophistication, and economic efficiency as well. The result, as Lawrence E. Harrison has written, is that the United States now emphasizes relatively cheap labor in the manner that Third World countries typically do. On the other hand, if the United States should make rapid progress in technological innovation, the ensuing reliance on robots and computers would ensure that a work force comprised significantly of uneducated and unskilled immigrants became to that extent unemployable and economically irrelevant. Robert Reich, secretary of labor in the Clinton administration, has warned that while an educated work force may well be able to attract global capital for its enterprises, an uneducated one could have the opposite effect: beckoned by low wages and low taxes elsewhere, international funds and technology can conceivably depress wages in formerly affluent countries to levels obtaining in the Third World. "Free immigration can be the death of free enterprise," Garrett Hardin warns. "When that goes, not much will remain of our other freedoms."

In the last several years the debate on the economic cost of immigration has flared anew, stimulated largely by "new findings" put forward by the Alexis de Tocqueville Institute, the Urban Institute, the Cato Institute, and especially by Stephen Moore, a Cato economist who was previously a senior economist at the Joint Economic Committee as an assistant to Representative Dick Armey, the congressman from Texas. Moore, who collaborated with Julian Simon in a number of economic studies related to immigration, is himself a sort of demi-Simon, never out of hearing of His Master's Voice playing endlessly in the background of his own work. Moore, who derides Pat Buchanan's and Governor Lamm's anti-immigrant "hysteria," insists that the significant difference between 1965 and today is that immigration from Europe has been heavily supplemented by immigration from Asia, so that the key issue becomes whether Asian immigrants help or do not help the U.S. economy. ". . . [M]ost research," he insists, "indicates a very high [economic] return from Cambodian, Chinese, Indian, Japanese, Pakistani, Taiwanese, and Vietnamese immigrants." More generally, Moore argues that as a result of demographic changes presently occurring in the American population, increased immigration to the United States until at least 2040 will be "more vital to the US national interest than at any time in recent history. . . . The US needs to admit more immigrants now to get us out of the demographic bind" created by the prospect of an aging population that threatens to bring down the Social Security system. (Ben Wattenberg has been pushing the demographic argument for close to a decade and a half.) Echoing Simon, Moore asserts that "Most research on immigrant use of welfare confirms the conclusion that immigrants are not much different in the use of social services than US-born citizens," and "Immigrants come to work, not to go on welfare.... Immigrants tend to have higher labor-force participation rates and tend to work longer hours than US-born residents."

Moore cites findings from 1985 by researchers for the Urban Institute purporting to show that, while immigrants to California take more money in social services than they pay in taxes, they are nevertheless a "significant economic asset" to their communities of residence, and draws attention to their conclusion that "the over-all economic benefits accruing to the average Los Angeles household from the presence of Mexican immigrants *probably* outweigh the economic costs of fiscal deficits." (My emphasis.) He reiterates Linda Chavez's dubious claim that immigrants "may save," as he phrases it, declining American industries including the fruit and vegetable businesses, furniture-making, and poultry raising, and especially those facing strong competition from imports, such as the garment industry. According to Moore, a study he conducted with Simon and Richard Sullivan in 1993 shows that *one* American worker is displaced for every thirty immigrants entering the country, though he admits that "In some industries immigrants have undeniably taken jobs from US-born citizens," adding, "It is quite possible that the primary impact of immigrant workers is on wage rates rather than on unemployment rates"; even so, "[m]ost research finds" that the one group whose wages *are* affected is comprised of earlier immigrant arrivals. Immigrants, Moore says, fill "vital niches" in the labor market. He claims that the decline in the number of skilled immigrants noted by George Borjas was reversed in the middle and late 1980s, and that anyway "the reduction in immigrants' skill levels and earnings appears to be offset by other positive attributes of arrivals," including their capabilities for "economic assimilation." Just because immigrants are unskilled doesn't mean they aren't desirable, he reminds us. Besides, the problem of skills can be solved by imposing skills-based criteria for admission! Moore denies that Americans are leaving the cities to escape the presence of immigrants, whom he credits with having prevented "catastrophic declines" in major urban areas, where they have aided economic recovery and stimulated "vitality." He calls the recruitment and retention of foreign-born faculty "essential" to the maintenance of high standards in American colleges and universities, lauds "brilliant" students from abroad, and praises the "remarkable level of achievement of the children of immigrants. . . ." "For more than a century, immigration has been a process by which America skims the cream of other nations' human capital." (Would Moore advocate "skimming" gold and diamonds from South Africa, tin and natural gas from Bolivia? This is neo-imperialism with a vengeance.)[37]

Stephen Moore has publicly mocked Donald Huddle and his analysis of the cost imposed by immigration upon the American public. But as Virginia Abernethy and Vernon Briggs pointed out in a letter to the *Washington Times* in 1995, critiques of Huddle's conclusions have been made almost without exception by immigrationist groups like the Urban Institute. The UI's analysis, they add, is itself flawed by obvious errors, such as crediting the employers' portion of the Social Security tax to the tax contribution paid by immigrants. "Mr. Huddle's work, on the contrary, has substance. Iterations of his analysis in three successive years have shown rising costs from the increasing stock of post-1970 immigrants in the United States. The current study showed $51 billion in 1994 public-sector costs, in excess of taxes paid by immigrants."[38]

The economic argument for immigration is in truth, as Fairchild thought, the principal one on its behalf. It is also the most compelling, though not compelling enough when weighed against the many strong arguments that have been made against immigration from the standpoint of other considerations. It is, finally, an outmoded argument, having nothing to offer an economically mature Western nation beset by unprecedented international strife and turmoil, and everything with which to threaten it.

NOTES

1. Ira Mehlman, "Reluctant Observers," *The Social Contract,* Spring 1994, p. 200.
2. Gregory Fossedahl, *The Democratic Imperative: Exporting the American Revolution* (New York: Basic Books, 1989), pp. 48, 240–41.
3. Cf. John O'Sullivan, "America's Identity Crisis," *National Review,* 21 November 1994, pp. 36–45, 76.
4. John Lukacs, *Outgrowing Democracy: A History of the United States in the Twentieth Century* (New York: Doubleday, 1984), p. 24.
5. Lawrence Auster, *The Path to National Suicide* (Monterey, Va.: American Immigration Control Foundation, 1990), p. 17.
6. Cf. Daniel A. Stein, "The Pros and Cons of Immigration: A Debate," *Chronicles: A Magazine of American Culture,* July 1990, p. 17.
7. Linda Seebach, "Proposition 187 Means Freedom," *Casper Star-Tribune,* 5 November 1994, p. A6.
8. Rita J. Simon and Susan Alexander, *The Ambivalent Welcome: Print Media, Public Opinion and Immigration* (Westport, Conn.: Praeger, 1993), p. 228.
9. John A. Scanlon and O. T. Kent, "The Force of Moral Arguments for a Just Immigration Policy in a Hobbesian Universe: The Contemporary American Example," in Mark Gibney, ed., *Open Borders? Closed Societies?* (New York: Greenwood Press, 1988), pp. 94–95.
10. Otis L. Graham, *Illegal Immigration and the New Reform Movement* (Washington, D.C.: Federation for American Immigration Reform, 1980), p. 29.

11. Anthony P. Maingot, "Ideology, Politics, and Citizenship in the American Debate on Immigration Policy: Beyond Consensus," in Mary M. Kritz, ed., *U.S. Immigration and Refugee Policy: Global and Domestic Issues* (Lexington, Mass.: Lexington Books, 1983), p. 29.

12. Frederick G. Whelan, "Citizenship and Freedom of Movement: An Open Admission Policy?" in Gibney, ed., *Open Borders?*, pp. 3–39.

13. John A. Scanlon and O. T. Kent, "The Force of Moral Arguments for a Just Immigration Policy in a Hobbesian Universe," in *Open Borders?*, pp. 63–64, 84–89.

14. Ibid., p. 93.

15. O'Sullivan, "America's Identity Crisis," p. 37.

16. Demetrios G. Papademetriou and Mark J. Miller, "Immigration Reform: The United States and Western Europe Compared," in Papedemetriou and Miller. eds., *The Unavoidable Issue: U.S. Immigration Policy in the 1980s* (Philadelphia: Institute for the Study of Human Issues, 1983), pp. 273–74.

17. Simon and Alexander, *The Ambivalent Welcome,* pp. 62, 87.

18. John Lukacs, *Immigration and Migration: A Historical Perspective* (Monterey, Va.: American Immigration Control Foundation, 1986), p. 2.

19. John Ney, *Miami Today—The U.S. Tomorrow* (Monterey, Va.: American Immigration Control Foundation, 1982), pp. 13–14.

20. Peter Brimelow, "Does the Nation-State Exist?" *The Social Contract,* Summer 1993, pp. 229–34; cf. William Hawkins, *Importing Revolution: Open Borders and the Radical Agenda* (Washington, D.C.: American Immigration Control Foundation/U.S. Business and Industrial Council Foundation, 1994), p. 105.

21. Gerda Bikales, "The Golden Rule in the Age of the Global Village," *The Social Contract,* Winter 1992–93, pp. 113–15.

22. Roy Beck, "Washington Notepad," *The Social Contract,* Summer 1993, p. 279.

23. Roy Beck, "Right of Silence?" *National Review,* 11 July 1994, pp. 32–34.

24. William Hawkins, *Importing Revolution,* Introduction by Samuel T. Francis, pp. vi, 102–8.
25. Ibid., p. 100.
26. Samuel Francis, "Principalities and Powers," *Chronicles,* July 1990, p. 11.
27. John Sullivan, "Immigration's Effects on Blacks," *The Social Contract,* Fall 1993, p. 40.
28. Hawkins, *Importing Revolution,* Introduction by Samuel T. Francis, p. ix.
29. "A New Establishmentarianism," *The Religion and Society Report,* April 1994, p. 5.
30. Lawrence Fuchs, "The Reactions of Black Americans to Immigration," in Virginia Yans-McLaughlin, ed., *Immigration Reconsidered: History, Sociology, and Politics* (New York: Oxford University Press, 1990), p. 293.
31. Glaister A. Elmer and Evelyn E. Elmer, *Ethnic Conflicts Abroad: Clues to America's Future?* (Monterey, Va.: American Immigration Control Foundation, 1988), p. 3.
32. "Religion and the Environment," *The Social Contract,* Winter 1992–93, pp. 76–89.
33. Cf. Matthew Welde, "The Theological and Political Aspects of Sanctuary," in Maria H. Thomas, ed., *Sanctuary: Challenge to the Churches* (Washington, D.C.: Institute on Religion and Democracy, 1986), pp. 59–60; also remarks by Bruce Nichols, p. 62.
34. Maingot, "Ideology, Politics, and Citizenship in the American Debate on Immigration Policy," pp. 374–75.
35. Michael S. Teitelbaum, *Latin Migration North: The Problem for U.S. Foreign Policy,* (New York: Council on Foreign Relations, 1985), pp. 45, 56.
36. Elizabeth A. Koed, "The Loss of Cheap Labor and Predictions of Economic Disaster," *The Social Contract,* Spring 1991, p. 127.
37. Vernon M. Briggs Jr., *Still an Open Door? U.S. Immigration Policy and the American Economy* (Washington, D.C.: The American University Press, 1994), pp. 75–167.
38. Virginia Abernethy and Vernon M. Briggs, Jr. letter to the *Washington Times,* 24 November 1995, p. A22.

In addition to those cited above, works consulted in the preparation of this section include Virginia Abernethy, *Population Politics: The Choices That Shape Our Future* (New York: Insight Books, 1993); Roy Beck, *Re-Charting America's Future: Responses to Arguments against Stabilizing U.S. Population and Limiting Immigration* (Petoskey, Mich.: Social Contract Press, 1994); David Bennett, *The Party of Fear: From Nativist Movements to the New Right in American History* (Chapel Hill: University of North Carolina Press, 1988); Katherine Betts, *Ideology and Immigration: Australia, 1976–1987* (Melbourne, Australia: Melbourne University Press, 1988); George F. Borjas, *Friends or Strangers? The Impact of Immigration on the U.S. Economy* (New York: Basic Books, 1990); M. E. Bradford, *Sentiment or Survival: Crisis in the Immigration Policy of the United States* (Washington, D.C.: American Immigration Control Foundation, 1984); Vernon M. Briggs Jr., *Mass Migration and the National Interest* (Armonk, N.Y.: M. E. Sharpe, 1992); Peter Brimelow, *Alien Nation: Common Sense about America's Immigration Disaster* (New York: Random House, 1995); Linda Chavez, *Out of the Barrio: Toward a New Politics of Assimilation* (New York: Basic Books, 1991); Alan Dowty, *Closed Borders: The Contemporary Assault on Freedom of Movement* (New Haven, Conn.: Yale University Press, 1987); Henry Pratt Fairchild, *Immigration: A World Movement and Its American Significance* (New York: Macmillan, 1913); Laura Fermi, *Illustrious Immigrants: The Intellectual Migration from Europe, 1930–41,* 2d ed. (Chicago: University of Chicago Press, 1971); Samuel T. Francis, *Smuggling Revolution: The Sanctuary Movement in America* (Washington, D.C.: Capital Research Center, 1986); Lawrence H. Fuchs, *The American Kaleidoscope: Race, Ethnicity, and the Civic Culture* (Hanover, N.H.: Wesleyan University Press/University Press of New England, 1990); Otis L. Graham, *Rethinking the Purposes of Immigration Policy* (Washington, D.C.: Center for Immigration Studies, 1991); Lindsey Grant, *Elephants in the Volkswagen: Facing the Tough Questions about Our Overcrowded Country* (New York: W. H. Freeman and Company, 1992); Andrew Hacker, *The End of the American Era* (New York: Atheneum, 1968); Garrett Hardin, *Living within Limits: Ecology, Economics, and Population Taboos* (New York: Oxford University Press, 1993), and *The Immigration Dilemma: Avoiding the Tragedy of the Commons* (Washington, D.C.: Federation for American Immigration Reform, 1995); Horace M. Kallen, *Culture and Democracy in the United States* (New York: Boni and Liveright, 1924); Kenneth L. Karst, *Belonging to America: Equal Citizenship and the Constitution* (New Haven, Conn.: Yale University Press, 1989); Jacqueline Kasun, *The War against Population: The Economics and Ideology of Population Control* (San Francisco: Ignatius Press, 1988); Paul Kennedy, *Preparing for the Twenty-first Century* (New York: Random House, 1993); Richard D. Lamm and Gary Imhoff, *The Immigration Time Bomb: The Fragmenting of America* (New York: Dutton, 1985); Lester D. Langley, *MexAmerica* (New York: Crown, 1988); Christopher Lasch, *The Revolt of the Elites and the Betrayal of Democracy* (New York: Norton, 1995), and *The True and Only Heaven: Progress and Its Critics* (New York: Norton, 1991); John Lukacs, *Outgrowing Democracy: A History of the United States in the Twentieth Century* (New York: Doubleday, 1984); Edward N. Luttwak, *The Endangered American Dream: How to Stop the United States from Becoming a Third World Country and How to Win the Geo-Economic Struggle for Industrial Supremacy* (New York: Simon & Schuster, 1993); Eugene McCarthy, *A Colony of the World: The United States Today* (New York: Hippocrene, 1992); Daniel Patrick Moynihan, *Pandaemonium* (New York: Oxford University Press, 1993); Brent A. Nelson, *Assimilation: The Ideal and the Reality* (Monterey, Va.: American Immigration Control Foundation, 1987), and *The Coming Triumph of Mexican Irredentism* (Monterey, Va.: American Immigration Control Foundation, 1984); Max Oelschlaeger, *Caring for Creation: An Ecumenical Approach to the Environmental Crisis* (New Haven, Conn.: Yale University Press, 1994); Moses Rischin, ed., *Immigration and the American Tradition* (Indianapolis, Ind.: Bobbs-Merrill, 1976); Arthur M.

Schlesinger Jr., *The Disuniting of America: Reflections on a Multi-cultural Society* (New York: Norton, 1992); Peter H. Schuck and Rogers M. Smith, *Citizenship without Consent: Illegal Aliens in the American Polity* (New Haven, Conn.: Yale University Press, 1986); David E. Simcox, ed., *U.S. Immigration in the 1980s: Reappraisal and Reform* (Boulder, Colo.: Westview Press, 1988); Julian Simon, *The Economic Consequences of Immigration* (Oxford, Eng. and New York: Basil Blackwell, 1989) and *How Do Immigrants Affect Us Economically?* (Washington, D.C.: Center for Immigration Policy and Refugee Assistance, 1985); Peter Skerry, *Mexican Americans: The Ambivalent Minority* (New York: The Free Press, 1993); Michael Walzer, *Spheres of Influence: A Defense of Pluralism and Equality* (New York: Basic Books, 1983); Ben J. Wattenberg, *The First Universal Nation: Leading Indicators and Ideas about the Surge of America in the 1990s* (New York: The Free Press, 1991); and Thomas Weyr, *USA: Breaking the Melting Pot* (New York: Harper & Row, 1988).

See also Virginia Abernethy, "Optimism and Overpopulation," *Atlantic Monthly,* December 1994; Elliot Abrams and Franklin S. Abrams, "Immigration Policy—Who Gets What and Why?" *The Public Interest* 38, no. 3, 1975; Peter Brimelow, "Time to Rethink Immigration?" *National Review,* 22 June 1992; Matthew Connelly and Paul Kennedy, "Must It Be the Rest against the West?" *Atlantic Monthly,* December 1994; James Fallows, "Immigration: How It's Affecting Us," *Atlantic Monthly,* November 1983; Robert D. Kaplan, "The Coming Anarchy," *Atlantic Monthly,* February 1994; and Jack Miles, "Blacks vs. Browns: Immigration and the New American Dilemma," *Atlantic Monthly,* October 1992.

Conclusion

The Failure of
American Immigration

G REAT BRITAIN, IT HAS BEEN SAID, BECAME AN EMPIRE in a fit of absentmindedness. And so far as the United States really *is* the first universal nation, it was by a series of fits of absence of mind that it became so. "We tend," Richard Rodriguez says, ". . . to celebrate immigrants after the fact." He is so right. In the same way, America neither planned nor hoped to become a pluralistic country, ahead of the fact. Multi-culturalism is the response to multicultural immigration, making the best of a bad deal to which nobody who counted was paying attention at the time. Rodriguez again: "America transforms into pleasure what it cannot avoid." But might have avoided.

Perhaps the least that can be said against immigration to the United States is that it has been a distraction from the nation's many and considerable problems, and a complication of them as well. An article in the *Overland Monthly* in 1923 called attention to the fact. "As a result of the growing heterogeneity society can scarcely make up its mind anymore save on matters of such elemental appeal as fire protection, sanctity of property, good roads and public improvements. The 'interests,' politicians, and the foreign nationalistic organizations play one element against another so that we are not getting on as we should." Seventy years later, the editor of *Chronicles: A Magazine of American Culture* made a similar point regarding something greater than good roads and public improvements: "Immigration per se has not been the major obstacle to America realizing her nationhood, but the presence of immigration made it impossible to deal with the real problem, which has been and continues to be the centralization of political, economic, and cultural power." Centralization destroyed the regional system of American communities already weakened by mass immigration, while immigration produced levels of cultural, ethnic, and racial diversity that gradually, almost imperceptibly, have partially deconstructed the American nation. For most of this the Old— not the New—Immigration is responsible.

If America owes multiculturalism to the New Immigration, the "culture war" is attributable to the failure of immigration as "an American tradition." Immigration is a failure because assimilation, contrary to national myth, never really occurred. And assimilation failed because (*a*) the complete accommodation by one culture to another is virtually impossible; (*b*) the immigrants never wished for full assimilation anyway; (*c*) immigrant resentment of the old American stock has always persisted; and (*d*) the political and intellectual culture of the founding and early republican eras was fundamentally incompatible with any that has been subsequently introduced. Lawrence Fuchs believes history validates the confidence the cultural pluralists of the 1920s had that the United States would be strengthened and unified by "immigrant-ethnic diversity." His view is shared by many contemporary observers who continue to endorse Crèvecoeur's romantic vision of "a new race of men." But *E pluribus unum* was pregnant with danger from the start, though that danger required a century or so to make itself apparent.

Immigrants can be taught their adoptive nation's history, its literature, and its customs. They cannot, however, experience its past in the way that a native of the same country, whose ancestors fought in the American Revolution, pioneered the West, or attended Princeton with Scott Fitzgerald and Edmund Wilson, can experience it. Nor can they, in the degree that their countries of origin differ from the found one, appreciate the meaning of that past. Lawrence Auster, differentiating the old immigrants from the new, post-1965 variety, reminds us that immigrants from eastern and southern Europe—Irving Berlin, George Gershwin, Louis B. Mayer, Frank Capra, Frederick Loewe, Ernst Lubitch, Billy Wilder, and Ben Hecht—not only created Hollywood but contributed the songs, music, plays, and films that have become the popular classics of America in the twentieth century. According to Auster, these men both identified with and expressed artistically "Anglo-American archetypes" of an immigrant-native culture, and in so doing re-created the American ideal in a powerful new idiom. It is debatable, however, whether the work these very talented men performed was an expression or a re-creation of those archetypes, rather than a commercial vulgarization and ideological exploitation of them. In the final decades of the nineteenth century and the early ones of the twentieth, it was immigrants and the sons of immigrants who fabricated the national preference for a kind of song never heard in America before, or anywhere else for that matter: music that had no roots, certainly, in American folk ballads and expressive lyrics.

Jeffrey Rosen in the *New Republic* has deplored the hundred-year period between the 1870s and the 1970s for the antialien laws that in his opinion besmirched it, "a grim record of the country's anxieties throughout the century...." The word "anxieties" suggests Richard Hofstatder's famous thesis: that American reaction since the Civil War has been a function of the status anxiety experienced by old-line Americans as a result of their economic and social displacement by later immigrant groups. For Hofstatder, anxiety was a symptom of mental ill health, which in turn indicated spiritual disease. In fact, these Americans of the old stock had real objective as well as subjective concerns, since by 1912 an urban, industrial, and largely immigrant culture had all but destroyed the old Victorian-American culture and with it rural Protestant America; while from 1912 to 1970 it proceeded, in James Lincoln Collier's phrase, to stand on its head a national morality that had once seemed fixed and permanent. Sociologists returning to Muncie, Indiana—"Middletown"—forty years after the Lynds made their famous study discovered the single significant change to be an increased "tolerance" on the part of students there: 39 percent, compared with 94 percent in 1929 and 1937, believed that "Christianity is the one true religion and all people should be converted to it." And surely it says much about the "progress" of the Commonwealth of Massachusetts between 1850 and 1995 that the man who best embodies the worst qualities (except Popery) attributed to the Irish immigrants by Boston Brahmins should be today, as for the past thirty-three years, its most popular and irremovable politician.

American thought and politics were changed and redirected forever by the roughly twenty-five thousand professionals, including teachers, who arrived as refugees from Europe before Pearl Harbor and who, in the opinion of Leo Strauss, subsequently effected the Europeanization of the culture of the United States. Laura Fermi—widow of Enrico—credited the émigrés with having encouraged American universities to stress the theoretical sciences over the practical ones. "A similar trend toward pure knowledge is seen in other fields: the humanities have acquired greater prominence, philosophy has expanded, and the teaching of other disciplines has become more theoretically oriented." In Fermi's estimation, these "illustrious immigrants" had their greatest impact upon American culture as teachers; "artists, musicians, and writers found almost as many niches in our schools as did scholars and scientists." Following the abortive revolutions of 1848 a wave of immigrant intellectuals known as the Forty-eighters arrived in the United States, most prominent among them the Germans, who were much more interested in remaking American culture to their taste than they were in being transformed by it. Of these Germans the most famous was Carl Schurz, whose most significant contribution to American life was to infect it with notions of Prussian bureaucracy and Prussian centralization. A century afterward, a later generation of émigrés from central and eastern Europe employed quasi-Marxist doctrines, thinly disguised as Americàn republicanism, to challenge and undermine traditional American concepts of personal liberty and self-reliance inherited from their British forebears. Whether these influences amounted to the sophistication and cosmopolitanization of a provincial civilization is not the point; what matters is the imposition of an alien supplicant culture upon the indigenous host one, which, whatever its shortcomings, represented the cultural and intellectual flowering of a unique and interesting people. David Bennett, the chronicler of nativism in America, finds it politically significant that both the New and the Religious Right have displayed no signs of nativist resentment or behavior, having replaced immigrants as the preferred enemy with the New Class and the secularist culture it espouses. But since the New Class is entirely responsible for America's current immigration crisis, the likelihood exists that the Right will eventually discern that connection and recover the nativist tradition.

Some years ago Norman Podhoretz, then the editor of *Commentary,* remarked that the American Civil War was as ancient and irrelevant to him as the War of the Roses, his own family having arrived in the United States at a considerably later date. As an aging generation of American writers, critics, and politicians regards America before 1865 and the first epoch of mass immigration as irrelevant and even in some sense contemptible, so perhaps a coming generation will view America before 1965 in the same way. While the immigrants of the late nineteenth and early twentieth centuries may be described as having achieved a fair degree of assimilation, can the same be said of their grandchildren and great-grandchildren, who in the last several decades have rediscovered their ethnic identities and pursued them throughout a range of social, cultural, and political rebellions? If immigration to America and the assimilation of immigrants to American social norms, cultural tastes, intellectual traditions, and civic habits were in fact a national success story, then, it seems to me, the contemporary debate over immigration—as with those preceding it—would not be taking place at all.

1 October 1995,
Kemmerer, Wyoming